VICTORIAN GLA

GEOFFREY WILLS

VICTORIAN GLASS

London
G. BELL & SONS LTD
1976

First published in 1976 by
G. Bell & Sons Ltd
York House, 6 Portugal Street
London WC2A 2HL

ISBN 0 7135 1949 5

© 1976 by Geoffrey Wills

Printed in Great Britain
by Ebenezer Baylis and Sons Ltd
The Trinity Press, Worcester, and London

Preface

Anyone who studies the industrial world of the Victorian age finds that it was as prolific in ideas as in their realization. This applies to the glass industry as much as to any other. The glass-makers ceaselessly devised new shapes, colours and types of decoration, albeit in many instances imitating imported goods, but in others original. Despite a heavy reliance on hand-craftsmanship, the surviving quantities of many varieties prove that a prodigious output was achieved.

In so far as it is possible, the subject is here dealt with chronologically, although the varying periods of time during which many objects and styles remained fashionable and saleable has occasioned some over-lapping. The solid research on the glass of the era was published by Hugh Wakefield in 1961, in his *19th Century British Glass*. All who follow in his pioneer footsteps must be no less indebted to his work than the present writer.

G.W.

Contents

	Preface	*page* v
1	The eighteen-forties	1
2	The Great Exhibition	14
3	The influence of Venice	27
4	Etching and Cameo-carving	40
5	Press-moulded and other late varieties	54
6	Nailsea-type glass	67
	Appendix: Victorian glass manufacture and decoration	72
	Bibliography	85
	Index	87

Plates

Between pages 20 and 21

1. Epergne ornamented with cutting, 1837
2. Goblet engraved with barley ears, 1837
3. Plaque commemorating the laying of the first stone of the Royal Exchange, London, 1842
4. Decanter and stopper cut with shaped panels, 1845
5. Portrait of Queen Victoria in moulded glass, 1845
6. Carafe painted in colours with water plants, 1847
7. Water jug painted in colours with water-lilies, 1848
8. Group of examples of Venetian-style glass, 1851
9. Wine-glass in the Venetian style, 1851
10. Goblet, double-walled and internally silvered, 1850
11. Pair of candlesticks of double-walled clear glass, internally silvered, overlaid with green and cut, 1850
12. Pair of vases of pale ruby glass overlaid with opaque white, painted, 1850
13. Bottle of ruby glass, mounted as a ewer, 1851
14. Pair of vases and a ewer of ruby glass, 1850
15. Pair of vases of cream-coloured glass painted with Grecian figures, 1850
16. Pair of two-handled vases of clear glass, painted, 1850
17. Vase of opaque white glass decorated in dark brown, 1850
18. Jug of matt-surfaced white opaline glass painted in sepia, 1850
19. Scent bottle inset with a cameo-incrustation, with stopper, 1850
20. Carafe engraved with vine leaves and grapes, 1855
21. Scent bottles, 1850–60
22. Pair of lustres of clear glass decorated with cutting, 1860
23. Lustre of ruby glass overlaid with opaque white, painted, 1860
24. Claret jug, engraved, 1872
25. Amphora of 'Early Italian design', engraved, 1860

PLATES

Between pages 36 and 37

26 'The Ailsa Jug', 1862
27 Jug of clear glass, engraved, 1860
28 Wine-glass engraved, 1860
29 Part of a table service, 1859
30 Comport, press moulded in clear glass, 1867
31 Fairy lamp for burning oil
32 Two-handled celery vase patterned with ferns, 1869
33 Goblet, engraved, 1877
34 Water jug with etched decoration, 1870
35 Cameo glass showing stages in its manufacture
36 Vase of claret-coloured and opaque white glass with cameo
37 Plaque in spinach-green and opaque white glass with cameo
38 Plaque by George Woodall, 1884
39 Scent bottle of ruby glass, carved, 1887
40 Two vases, late-nineteenth century
41 Bowl of pink glass overlaid with white and patterned, late-nineteenth century
42 Vase of olive-green overlaid and patterned, late-nineteenth century
43 Scent bottles with cameo decoration, 1889
44 Vase of 'Ivory Cameo', etched and engraved, 1880
45 Basket of clear glass shading to green, 1880
46 Pair of vases of vari-coloured glass overlaid with clear, late-nineteenth century
47 Jar and cover of ruby-coloured glass, late-nineteenth-century
48 Bowl and cover of topaz-coloured glass enclosing swirling white tapes, late-nineteenth century
49 Pot of opalescent white glass, spattered in various colours, late-nineteenth century

Between pages 52 and 53

50 Vase and jug of milk-white glass with applied coloured ornament, late-nineteenth century
51 Flower holder in opalescent topaz-coloured glass, late nineteenth century
52 Vase, shading in colour with a satin finish, enamelled and gilt, 1880

PLATES

53 Jug of opaque white over clear glass overlaid with blue, and with satin surface, 1880
54 Vase of Queen's Burmese ware, 1890
55 Table centrepiece with flower holders and nightlights in Queen's Burmese ware, 1890
56 Chandelier in clear glass decorated with ruby and green, 1865
57 Decanter in green-tinted glass, 1870
58 Flower vase with fan-shaped bowl, 1880
59 Venetian style glass, 1876
60 Champagne glass in Venetian style, 1876
61 Vase of clear glass partially layered, and engraved, 1885
62 Vase engraved in Rock Crystal style, 1885
63 Two specimen flower holders in clear glass
64 Dish in colourless glass, press-moulded, mid-nineteenth century
65 Dish for grapes, press-moulded in opaque white glass with satin finish, 1875
66 Flower vase of transparent blue glass, 1880
67 Three pieces of press-moulded cream-coloured ware, 1880
68 Vase, press-moulded in marbled glass, 1880
69 Vase, press-moulded in variegated glass, 1882
70 Receptacle in the form of a basket, press-moulded, 1880
71 Sugar basin in opalescent yellow glass, 1891
72 Dish in colourless glass, press-moulded, 1887
73 Two boats of press-moulded glass
74 Vase with vertically-ribbed body and handles, 1880
75 Jug of bubbles and spotted glass, 1880
76 Vase made of glass with opalescent streaks, bubbles and chemical inclusions, 1870
77 Set of six tumblers and jug in clear glass with silver mounts, 1882
78 Two rolling-pins
79 Flask of striped glass with pewter mount and screw cap
80 Five coloured glass hand-bells

I

The eighteen-forties

In England, during the second half of the eighteenth century, glassware ornamented with cutting became widely popular. At first, cutting was in the form of shallow slices that could be executed without calling for articles with thicker walls than normal. Before long, however, the cutters improved their technique and increased the range of designs; whereas glass had formerly been admired for its likeness to natural rock crystal, the new criterion was its capacity to glitter in the manner of a diamond. To achieve this effect, the English lead or flint glass, introduced by George Ravenscroft in the late seventeenth century, proved admirable. For the deep cutting that duly became fashionable a heavily-made article was essential, and some of the finished objects were so weighty and so bristling with jagged points that they could scarcely be handled under ordinary conditions.

The brilliant appearance of this English glassware was appreciated not only by home buyers, but by others farther afield, and a large export trade grew up to supply purchasers on the mainland of Europe and in the Americas and the Indies. Factories for producing similar goods were established in France and the Netherlands, and from the early 1780s several English makers operated from glasshouses set up at Waterford and elsewhere in Ireland. In that country, glassware and other manufactured products were tax-free between 1780 and 1825, enabling a large proportion of the output to be sold competitively on the far side of the Atlantic and in other countries.

By the first decade of the nineteenth century the public had acquired a taste for thick-walled glassware in spite of the duty levied on it in England. The state of affairs was paralleled in silver: the substantial productions of Paul Storr and his contemporaries, similarly taxed by weight, were the height of fashion despite their cost. Extravagance was the order of the day.

As early as 1785 Horace Walpole had referred, with sarcasm, to 'Mr

Adam's gingerbread and sippets of embroidery', and later, in 1800, George III contributed to the criticism by saying: 'I am a little of an architect and think that the old school is not enough attended to – the Adams have introduced too much of neatness and prettiness. . . .' The revolt against the graceful forms and delicate ornamentation introduced by Robert Adam grew in volume, to be expressed finally by another architect, Charles Heathcote Tatham. He published in 1806 a book of silverware designs in which he stated in the Foreword: 'It has been lamented by Persons high in Rank, and eminent for Taste, that modern Plate has fallen much in design and execution from that formerly produced in this Country. Indeed, the truth of this remark is obvious, for instance of *Massiveness*, the principal characteristic of good Plate, light and insignificant forms have prevailed, to the utter exclusion of all good Ornament whatever.' The key word was the one printed by its author in italic type, *Massiveness*, and while his message was directed to silversmiths, who heeded it, it was also taken to heart and endorsed by glass-makers.

As mentioned briefly, glass produced in England was subject to a duty. When Princess Victoria succeeded her uncle, William IV, to the throne following his death on 20 June 1837, the industry was still labouring under an excise that had been levied continuously since 1745. In that year it had been at the rate of 9s. 4d. (47p) for clear or flint glass, and 2s. 4d. (12p) for coarse bottle-glass. As time passed the charges were gradually raised, until in 1813 they stood at £4 16s. (£4·80) for flint glass and 8s. 2d. (41p) for bottle-glass; the duty being payable throughout on every hundredweight (112 lb) of the material. Further modifications took place in succeeding years, and in 1826 every glasshouse was in addition required to be licensed annually at a cost of £20.

The duty was collected in a clumsy and costly manner, which was seized on by the makers as an important ground for its abolition. In 1654 a comparatively small tax had been levied on glass by William III, but the individual members of the industry had banded together and protested with such vigour that it was halted after five years. Possibly the memory of this success kept the fires of protest well stoked from 1745 onwards, for there was an almost unceasing condemnation voiced loudly throughout the duration of the impost.

The difficulty of manufacturing under the conditions imposed by Parliament was put into bitter words by Harry J. Powell of the Whitefriars glassworks, London, who was understandably somewhat biased when describing the tribulations of his forbears and their contemporaries. In 1923, long after the hated duty had been removed, he wrote: 'The sites only remain of the sentry-boxes in which the "officers of excise" spent such of their time in sleep as was not occupied in harrying the works' managers or being harried by the glasshouse boys. Two, at least, of these officers were quartered in every glass-works, and as the duty was payable partly on the worked and partly on the unworked glass, it was their business to register the total weight of glass melted and to prevent the removal of any piece of manufactured glass which had not been weighed.'

Following a rise in duty in 1812 it was observed that there was a considerable fall in production: in the region of 35 per cent in the period from 1813 to 1815 compared with that of 1810 to 1812. Evasion of the excise increased as the years passed, and it grew more worthwhile to avoid payment. Numerous small furnaces sited in out-of-the-way places were worked in secret, being known as 'cribs' or 'little-goes', producing goods of indifferent quality for quick sale at low prices. The men operating them used ingredients that melted easily and were inexpensive, adding to them plenty of old broken glass; a material known as cullet, that possessed both attributes. It was said that the operators of cribs had almost a monopoly at one period in supplying small bottles for use by chemists and others, as well as other goods on which good quality materials and sophisticated techniques would have been wasted.

The duty-gatherers called down on themselves the dislike of the glasshouse owners not only for their exactions and their disruption of daily routine, but because they also stifled change. Whether sold or not, all glass produced was subject to the tax, so that attempts to improve methods or materials were extra-costly and experiment thereby discouraged. In addition, the regulations confined each glasshouse to the making of any one type of glass to the exclusion of all others. It was difficult under the circumstances to meet competition from abroad, where the introduction of new ideas was continual, and which found a market eager for novelty. The Government finally took action, and in 1833 a Royal Commission was appointed to inquire into the industry.

The Commissioners held their meetings to take evidence and in due course reported to Parliament. They found that the loud and unceasing complaints of the manufacturers were largely justified and that, in brief, the excise impeded research and hindered, if not completely prevented, competition with an increasing quantity of imported goods. They gave their opinion that evasion of payment could not be legally countered with any hope of success, and in any case the cost of collection of unpaid duty would probably outweigh the resulting sum total.

Some slight action was taken, but the industry continued to stagnate for a further decade or so. Governments in most countries and at most periods have shared an aversion to altering a *status quo*; an understandable caution gained from experiencing the unsuspected effects of sudden change. Official passivity in the matter of glass duty was no exception, and reluctance to make a move was doubtless encouraged by those employed in administering the cumbrous system. After having been in operation for a hundred years it had become as well established as the industry on which it lived, and the duty-gatherers not unnaturally foresaw any changes, other than further rises in the duty, as being certain to affect them adversely.

The industry itself was little less hidebound. By the 1840s cut clear glass had been an English speciality for so long that its making had reached a very high standard, and the manufacturers were well organized to fill the demand for such goods. Employers as well as craftsmen were loath to alter their ways; a naturally conservative outlook allied with the restrictive taxation resulted in an almost complete lack of initiative in making innovations. In the early years of Queen Victoria's reign, even if the shapes of many glass articles differed from those of preceding decades their ornamentation was much the same. Cutting prevailed over all else, as it had done earlier, although it varied from time to time in details of its design.

A handbill issued by a provincial dealer in the 1840s lists his stock at the time. Although it only hints at the appearance of items, it details the comprehensive range available and makes it manifest that cutting was a desirable feature. The relevant portion of the notice reads: 'Rich Cut and Plain Glass Decanters, Water Caraffes [sic], Wine Coolers, Finger Cups, elegant Cut Trifle Dishes, Celery Glasses, Water and Cream Jugs, Sugar and Cream Basins, Butter Tubs, Bee Hives and Pickle Glasses, Sets of Castors, Spirit Bottles, Toilet Bottles, Cruets, Mustards, and Salts, Inkstands, Bird-fountains and Boxes, Cut

Champagne, Claret, Hock and Wine Glasses, Rich Cut Goblets and Tumblers, Jelly and Custard Cups, Cut Ales, Beer Tumblers, Exciseman's Inks, Fish Globes, Show Glasses, Eye Glasses, Passage Lamps, French Domes and Lamps, with a variety of other articles and Fancy Ornaments.'

The goods listed above were offered for sale by an unnamed advertiser trading at an address named 'Staffordshire House', in Lemon Street, a principal thoroughfare in Truro, Cornwall. The name was doubtless bestowed on the premises because various kinds of earthenware were included in the stock, but it is not improbable that the glass originated not very far from the Potteries: at Stourbridge, in Worcestershire, just across the river Stour that divides the county from neighbouring Staffordshire.

Stourbridge has traditionally been said to have been the site of glass-making activities since the mid-sixteenth century, when some immigrants from Lorraine, in northern France, first settled there. An alternative theory is that Hungarian refugees were responsible for establishing the industry, and to confirm their existence it was said that they settled themselves 'on an eminence just outside the town, known to this day as Hungary Hill'. Support for the Lorrainers lies in the continued presence in the glass trade, from about 1570 onwards, of men with French surnames. These included Thisac and Hennezel, which subsequently became anglicized as Tyzack and Henzey or Ensell.

If, as is likely, the Frenchmen came to Stourbridge in the second half of the sixteenth century, they would have done so for two reasons. First, they had aroused jealousy among the inhabitants of Sussex and other southern areas where they first settled and secondly there was increasing Government concern at the inroads in timber supplies being caused by makers of glass and iron. In 1615, James I decreed that glassmakers should no longer burn wood in their furnaces, and Stourbridge lay conveniently close to ample supplies of coal. Additionally, there were local deposits of a clay that was ideal for making the large pots in which the ingredients of glass were melted. During the eighteenth century the town became linked by canal with many parts of England, and its commercial prosperity was thereby assured. By 1831 it was reported that there were then 'twelve glass houses in the immediate neighbourhood, in which the different varieties of flint, crown, bottle, and window glass, are manufactured, besides cutting mills'. In the course of the remainder of the century Stourbridge became the principal centre of English glass-making.

In the 1840s there were a number of centres of glass production. Manchester boasted Molineaux, Webb & Co., who started operations in about 1825, and whose output by 1850 had reached an annual total of 250 tons. The various establishments, large and small, in the region of Newcastle upon Tyne, famed throughout the eighteenth century for their window glass and distinctive wine glasses, continued to be active during the succeeding century. Bristol, which had enjoyed a very prosperous glass industry during the reign of George III and earlier, declined in importance, and by the time Victoria ascended the throne output was confined to wine bottles. It was a Bristol firm, James Powell & Sons who, in the mid-1830s, bought the old-established Whitefriars glassworks, off Fleet Street and no great distance from the site of the first successful English glasshouse started at Crutched Friars in 1570. The old Falcon glassworks, Blackfriars, was owned from about 1820 by Apsley Pellatt, son of a glass-dealer of the same name. At first the business was operated in partnership as Green & Pellatt, precedence being neatly balanced by trading from the firm's warehouse at St Paul's Churchyard with the names in reverse order, thus: Pellatt & Green. In due course both styles were replaced by Apsley Pellatt & Co. The younger Pellatt was an early historian of glass manufacture, and included in his career a period from 1852 to 1857 during which he was Member of Parliament for Southwark. Also, in the Midlands, Birmingham housed a number of firms active during most of the nineteenth century; that of Chance Bros specializing in sheet glass and being responsible for many innovations in its manufacture.

In the far north, in Scotland, Edinburgh was the home of the Caledonian Glass Works, later known as the Holyrood Flint Glass Works. Under the direction of John Ford, nephew of the founder of the business, it prospered, and in 1837 Ford was appointed Manufacturer to the Queen. To commemorate the accession, the firm made a large and impressive cut glass epergne (Plate 1), which possibly earned Royal approval and must certainly have served as an excellent advertisement. It can be criticized as an example of the excessive lengths to which cutters could go when given a free reign, leaving not a square millimetre of surface untouched and almost concealing the form of the article in a blaze of points of reflected light.

Almost all glass of the period from 1840 to 1850 was sold without any indication of the maker, and only in exceptional instances are origins traceable. Shapes and decorative styles are somewhat easier to define, and although dated examples are scarce and limited in range they are among the best guides to what was popular at a particular time. The majority of surviving examples, probably because more of them were made, are drinking vessels of various types, of which the goblet in Plate 2 is an example. Dated September 1837, three months after Victoria had become Queen, it is sufficiently distinctive to enable other pieces to be attributed to about the same year; always allowing for the fact that fashions sometimes endured over a period of as much as a decade, and occasionally longer. The goblet has a heaviness in the appearance of the short stem and the series of mouldings above the foot, while the shape of the bowl, perhaps to be described as an inverted flat-based pear, is noticeable. The decoration was cut on the wheel, but only lightly on account of the wall of the bowl being made sufficiently thin for the vessel to be usable. Decanters of the same period often follow a comparable form, only in their case the pear-shape, also flat-based, is not inverted. They were frequently cut with lancet panels round the body and with the stopper rising to a spire-like point, both features giving the whole a Gothic air.

In the first decades of the century an outbreak of experimentation had occurred in Bohemia, now a part of Czechoslovakia. The craft of glass-making had for long been traditional in an area where wood fuel and the necessary sand and other materials were plentiful, and there were enough workers to acquire the essential skills. The type of glass made there could not compete effectively with the brilliant English cut wares, and in self-defence – possibly also as a fashion reaction against clear transparency – there came a great flush of bright colours. One after another the factories produced their specialities: opalescent green and yellow, named *Annagrün* and *Annagelb*, from Josef Riedel's glasshouses in the Isergebirge; a sealing-wax red and a gold-decorated dense black known as *Hyalith*, from the Count von Buquoy's manufactories in the area of Gratzen; and *Lithyalin*, a near-opaque many-coloured marbled glass, from Frederick Egermann's establishment at Blottendorf. Some of these bore scarcely any resemblance to glass and might in many instances be mistaken for natural stone or glazed pottery and porcelain, but they were new and colourful and were bought eagerly in England and elsewhere.

From the mid-1820s, also in pursuit of change, the French put on the market a variety of glass later named *Opaline*, which bears a resemblance to blancmange. After spending the preceding half-century producing good and bad imitations of English cut wares, the French glass industry slowly came to life, and Opaline was one of its successes. As early as the year 1612 an Italian, Antonio Neri, had published a book containing a formula for making a glass 'the colour of milk', and others were printed at later dates. Material of the kind was made at various times in several countries: in Venice and England it was employed as an effective near-substitute for porcelain, but most commonly articles of indifferent quality with garish painted decoration were made from it. It was the French who improved this milk-glass, referred to it as *cristal opalin* and produced from it a variety of useful and ornamental articles in pale hues of blue, pink, lilac, green, yellow and off-white. It proved before long to be no less acceptable to the public than the rival and quite different Bohemian wares, and the early examples of Opaline, which were frequently sold in mounts of gilt bronze, have never lost their international appeal.

From the date of its first imposition in 1745, the glass-makers had agitated against the duty on their products, and following the report of the Royal Commission of 1833 they did not slacken their efforts to publicize their grievances. During the next few years the duty was lowered until it stood at no more than three farthings (less than $\frac{1}{2}$p) per pound for flint glass, but nothing less than complete abolition would satisfy the industry. Finally, on 5 April 1845 this came about, the relevant Acts were repealed and freedom was at last regained.

Immediately, one of the Stourbridge firms sent a revised list of prices to its customers, warning them that 'the reduction of duty cannot influence the price of Flint and Cut Glass to any extent', and informing them that its own goods would be lowered by one penny (less than $\frac{1}{2}$p) in the pound weight. It may be suspected that the glass-makers had been protesting for so long that they had continued to do so after the cause had been largely removed. On the other hand, the actual payment of the money must have been a minor matter weighed against the irritating inconvenience of its collection. One of the makers made this clear in his evidence before the 1833 Commission:

'Our business and our premises are placed under the arbitrary control of a class of men to whose will and caprice it is most irksome to have to submit, and this under a system of regulations most ungraciously inquisitorial. We cannot enter parts of our premises without their permission; we can do no one single act without having previously notified our intention to the officers placed over us.'

Once they were free of restraint the English makers set about competing with the coloured wares that had become increasingly fashionable during the preceding score of years. Coloured glass was not new to the industry, although it had not been produced in any great quantity for a long time. The so-called 'Bristol Blue', which was by no means a monopoly of the seaport's glasshouses, and amethyst, green and yellow were produced from at least 1750, but only in comparatively small amounts.

When he was at Stourbridge in 1751 the peripatetic cleric, Dr Richard Pocock, noted that the town was: '. . . famous for its glass manufactures, especially its coloured glass, with which they make painted windows, which is here coloured in the liquid, of all the capital colours in their several shades. . . .' A few years later, in 1758, James Dossie's book, *The Handmaid to the Arts*, gave all who cared to read it full details of the ingredients required for a wide range of coloured glasses.

In the next century, such glass was not at first popular, but it is known that in 1837 Powell's of Whitefriars presented Queen Adelaide with a pair of yellow girandoles 'coloured by a salt of uranium'. The employment of this chemical for the purpose was new in England, its most successful application to date having been in Bohemia where it was used in making *Annagelb* and *Annagrün*. There are also records of the Stourbridge firm of W. H., B. & J. Richardson having made various coloured goods from about 1840.

With the demise of the duty there was a large-scale move in the glass industry to catch up with the French and Bohemians, if not to beat them at their own game. For some time, Robert Lucas Chance had owned window-glass factories at Nailsea, near Bristol, and Smethwick, near Birmingham, and being anxious to improve both quality and output he had obtained the collaboration of Georges Bontemps, manager of a glassworks at Choisy-le-Roi, outside Paris. The latter was greatly interested in the making of coloured glass, especially coloured sheet glass, and his discoveries in connection with this proved valuable. They were readily applicable to other products, being of considerable assistance to makers of useful and ornamental wares.

When Louis-Philippe was overthrown in 1848, Bontemps, along with many other skilled men, left France. He joined Chance's staff, devoting much of his time to devising glasses suitable for lenses, there being a big demand for them for use in telescopes and microscopes, and for the recently-invented camera. Bontemps committed his knowledge and experience to paper, publishing a book, *Le Guide du Verrier*, in 1868.

Not only were there successful attempts to produce a range of good colours, but earlier processes were improved and brought into use. One of these was press-moulding, which had been attempted earlier and subsequently developed in the United States. By 1831 it was known in England and was soon afterwards being employed by firms at Stourbridge and Birmingham. Goods produced by pressing were not to be compared with those made by traditional hand methods, but had the paramount advantage of cheapness; they could be made in very large quantities by semi-skilled labour, and were superficially attractive enough in appearance and low enough in price to sell on a large scale.

Early pressed wares have mostly vanished long ago, their low price and workaday finish causing them to be treated casually and discarded without thought. Information about what was made by the process in the first half of Victoria's reign depends mainly on scanty references that appeared in print at the date of manufacture. Thus, in 1848, George B. Sander, of High Holborn, London, advertised that he held the largest stock of china and glass in the capital. It included: 'Cut quart decanters, 10s. pair; cut wine-glasses, 4s. dozen; pressed tumblers, 4s. 6d. ditto; cut ditto, 5s. 6d. ditto.' Present-day shoppers may consider the difference in price of one shilling (5p) between pressed and cut tumblers a trifling matter. In fact it is nearly 20 per cent, and as the century advanced the gulf between the cost of the good and the commonplace gradually widened.

Other techniques were developed in emulation of imported wares. The old style of all-over cutting was largely rendered superfluous by the use of colour, on which such work was wasted. By using casing or overlaying, with one or more colours superimposed over a clear base, cutting could reveal the successive layers effectively, being particularly attractive when 'windows' were given bevel-edged framing.

Such work was often further embellished with painting and gilding to give the finished article a look of richness, if not of ostentation.

Some of the critics at the time did not consider that the English glassware reached the standard of that from Bohemia, and in addition it was pointed out that the former was more costly. However, provided that the resemblance to the imported articles was sufficiently close, it is very doubtful if buyers cared. So long as the goods on sale were fashionable their origin was of little or no interest to the majority of purchasers, who were content to be in the mode.

Many of the patterns on glass of the 1840s showed signs of Gothic influence, whether the designs were cut or otherwise applied. It was the use of conjoined arches and other motifs on articles for everyday use that was roundly castigated by the architect, A. W. N. Pugin, who considered that churches should be the sole beneficiaries where Gothic ornament was concerned. In his book, *True Principles of Pointed or Christian Architecture*, published in 1841, he did not specifically mention glassware, but doubtless it was included in his general condemnation of contemporaneous chattels. Pugin wrote: 'Glaring, showy, and meretricious ornament was never so much in vogue as at present; it disgraces every branch of our art and manufactures, and the correction of it should be an earnest consideration of every person who desires to see the real principles of art restored.'

Quite soon after those lines had appeared in print there were the first signs of a movement to improve design, and combat the low standard to which it had fallen; a condition due to the increasing momentum of the Industrial Revolution and its replacement of man by machinery. If any one person can be said to have been responsible for the fresh appraisal of design it was the Prince Consort, Albert of Saxe-Coburg-Gotha, whom Queen Victoria had married in 1840. Three years later the Prince agreed to become President of the Society of Arts, and was duly elected. The Society had been founded in 1754, had done much useful work, and undoubtedly the acquisition of a Royal president in 1843 awoke it from a torpor into which it had lapsed.

The Society initiated a series of annual exhibitions at which prizes were offered for the best examples in each class of goods shown. The first two, held in 1844 and 1845, were on a small scale, attracted only slight attention and information about them is meagre. A further attempt on the same lines took place in 1846, when one of the prize-winning entries was a china teaset made by the Staffordshire firm of Minton's to the design of 'Felix Summerly'. The latter was the pseudonym of Henry (later, Sir Henry) Cole, an energetic man who played an important part in artistic affairs during much of the remainder of the century. Following receipt of the award, he realized that there were commercial possibilities in carefully-designed and well-made articles with qualities superior to those available in the shops.

Cole gathered together a number of artists and manufacturers and in 1847, with himself as business manager, launched the firm of Summerly's Art Manufactures. Various articles in china and silver were favourably received by the public, and at least one pattern of glassware has survived. The water carafe in Plate 6 was made for Summerly's by J. F. Christy, who had a glassworks in Lambeth, and bears a design of water plants by Richard Redgrave. Its success can be gauged by the fact that in the following year the same appropriate theme was used by the Stourbridge firm that made a water jug patterned with waterlilies (Plate 7).

Cole's method of business was to commission the designs, hand them on to the chosen makers and leave the latter to do the selling. The manufacturers were responsible for the total expense from start to finish, but Cole made his own contribution in the form of publicity and his firm charged a royalty on all sales. As Cole had by then become a member of the Council of the Society of Arts he was in a strong position to ensure that the goods featured in their annual exhibitions. He was also able to make certain that they were not overlooked by the press in addition to their being admired by the public.

It has been stated that the Summerly tea service 'originated the application of art to industry'. Certainly it led in a more or less direct route to the Great Exhibition of 1851, in which Cole was to play a prominent part. In order to attend to its preparation he abandoned the Art Manufactures, but in any case it would appear that the manufacturers and the press had by then withdrawn support for the project. The former because the finished goods did not invariably please the public and so provide a worthwhile profit; the latter, it is said, as an expression of disapproval at Cole's exploitation of the resources of the Society of Arts.

The late 1840s saw the British public being offered two quite different styles of home-manufactured glasswares from which to make a choice.

There were the articles slavishly and conservatively following earlier native styles or imitating as closely as possible the more recent ones from Bohemia. Alternatively, there was the more thoughtfully conceived work of a few men who foresaw that the machine was close to killing all artistic expression, and that steps must be taken to thwart this. It was a contest of ideas continuing throughout the nineteenth century into the twentieth, and remaining relevant today.

2

The Great Exhibition

The year 1851 is an important reference point in studying manufactures of all kinds, including glass. It was the year in which was held the Great Exhibition of the Works of Industry of All Nations, to give it its full title, sited in Hyde Park, London. The exhibition was extensively documented at the time, with the official catalogue running to four heavy volumes containing over 1,500 pages plus illustrative plates. There were also numerous other publications equally helpful in evoking the occasion, not least among them the journal of Queen Victoria, who performed the opening ceremony on 1 May 1851.

The glass-making industry in England received what was undoubtedly its greatest advertisement by the decision to accept Joseph Paxton's design for the exhibition building. This was, in effect, a gigantic greenhouse constructed of iron clad in sheet glass. The latter was supplied by Chance's of Birmingham, and comprised an estimated 293,655 panes with a total weight in the region of 400 tons. When it was only half completed the edifice earned itself an appropriate name: a writer in *Punch* dubbed it the 'Crystal Palace', which its glittering appearance on sunny or rainy days alike must have fully merited.

All the British exhibitors of glass, as well as those from farther afield, whether they showed clear or coloured examples, seldom if at all displayed it unadorned. Each piece was decorated in some manner or other: cutting vied with painting or the two were combined, and in addition there was plenty of gilding. Much of the elaborate ornamentation was instigated by the circumstances, in which international rivalry was inherently encouraged. The entrants from each participating country sent of their best, and in the majority of instances this took the form of the most remarkable of its kind with the object of catching the eye of as many as possible of the thousands of visitors thronging the building. The pieces on display, therefore, were all too often exaggerated examples of what might be seen in the shops and available for purchase by the public. In retrospect, allowing for such distortion, the often over-sized and over-ornamented exhibits enable an assessment to be made of the makers' skill, even if their taste and motive are open to argument.

Much of the printed matter in connection with the event comprises written descriptions, catalogue entries as well as critical appraisals. A proportion of the many exhibits was illustrated, but photography was still in its infancy and confined in the main to recording human beings or scenery. Small-sized, everyday objects of glass or any other material, for use or ornament, were seldom faced with the lens, and other processes were employed to depict them. A few of the more striking articles displayed in the exhibition, as well as exterior and interior views of the building, were photographed by the recently devised Calotype process. This yielded paper negatives from which any number of prints might be made. Others were taken by Daguerreotype, permitting no multiplication and surviving originals are very rare. In either instance, printed reproductions in quantity were obtainable at the time only by the hand-processes of engraving on copper or steel, by lithography or by woodcut; the latter possessing the distinct advantage that it could be printed in one with the text, whereas engraved plates and lithographs required separate printing.

The majority of surviving visual records are in the form of woodcuts, which must be accepted as better than nothing. Woodcuts are seldom completely satisfactory for conveying an exact likeness of an object: it is difficult to render a fluent line in the medium, and although many excellent craftsmen practised the art of woodblock-cutting they only occasionally produced more than an approximation to a subject that they had almost certainly not actually seen. Therefore, these old illustrations must be viewed with a sympathetic eye, and a realization that many of the articles they depict were less unpleasing to look at than might be thought to be the case. Comparison of some of the few exhibits that have survived unscathed since 1851 with their portrayals at the time they were made demonstrates this clearly (Plates 8 and 9).

The display of English glass at the exhibition was contributed by about 100 makers and agents, and ranged from watch-glasses to a crystal fountain standing 27 ft (8·23 m) in height. Also shown on the same debatable premise that 'bigger is better' was a chandelier for 144 candles and a pair of fifteen-light candelabra. These last stood some 8 ft (2·43 m) high, had been a birthday gift to Prince Albert from the Queen in 1849 and may be seen today at Osborne House.

The introductory notes in the glass section of the catalogue, printed above the initials R.E., noted that the material: '. . . is beginning to assume an extraordinary degree of importance in the present day. Yet few manufactures have, until within a very recent period, made so small an amount of progress. Every process of the manufacturer having been beset with the stringent regulations considered to be necessary to enforce the due observance of the Excise laws, and no exemption being permitted even for the purpose of experiment or improvement, it is scarcely a matter of surprise that the production of glass remained in a poor and imperfect state both as a manufacture and as a philosophical problem. The same causes now no longer existing, a vast amount of progress has been made both in the extensions of the applications of this product, and also in the process of manufacture.'

These descriptions, although only brief, given in the lists of exhibits prove that the last sentence was by no means a mis-statement. For example, Rice Harris & Son, of the Islington Glass Works, Birmingham, showed the following: 'Ornamental glass of various colours, opal, alabaster, turquoise, amber, canary, topaz, chrysoprase, pink, blue, light and dark ruby, black, brown, green, purple, &c., coloured by oxides of copper and gold.

'The articles made in these colours are gilt, enamelled, cut, and engraved; they consist of tazzas, liqueur services, compotiers, butter-coolers, sugar-basins, toilet-bottles, claret-jugs, goblets, water-jugs, vases, &c.'

The same firm also showed thread-decorated pieces: 'a kind of glass for which Venice is famous, and where it was for a long time almost exclusively manufactured'. Harris's were, it would seem, the sole exhibitors of pressed goods of which they listed: 'Pressed and moulded glass tumblers, goblets, wines, sugar-basins, butter-coolers, salt-cellars, honey-pots, door knobs, &c.'

Other important firms of the day had comparable exhibits. They included George Bacchus & Sons, F. & C. Osler, and Lloyd & Summerfield, all of Birmingham; W. H., B. & J. Richardson, Davis, Greathead & Green, and Thomas Webb, all of Stourbridge; Molineaux, Webb & Co., of Manchester; and J. G. Green of St James's Street, and

Apsley Pellatt & Co., of Southwark, both of London. Of them all, J. G. Green and Osler's showed only cut clear glass, the latter firm being responsible for the great fountain that formed a centre of attraction. The others included in their displays greater or lesser proportions of coloured wares.

Cut clear glass was shown also by George Gatchell, owner of the Irish Waterford glassworks. With the imposition in Ireland of a duty on glass in 1825, the hitherto tax-free production was curtailed and the majority of the once busy makers soon discovered that they were no longer able to compete successfully in the open market. By the time George Gatchell took over at Waterford in 1848 the concern had been running for sixty-five years, and although it was far from being as prosperous as it had once been it was doing its best to remain solvent. In 1851 came an opportunity to prove how well it was maintaining the quality of glass and craftsmanship for which it had been known for so long.

The Waterford display included an elaborate 'centre stand for a banqueting table', with forty cut dishes and other pieces. All fitted together and had been designed in such a way that no metal or material other than glass was needed for the purpose of assembling the article. There was also a selection of decanters, and a 'Centre vase, or bowl, on detached tripod stand'. No doubt it all glittered bravely and was admired, but in vain. Before the exhibition closed its doors for the last time on 15 October 1851, Gatchell had been declared bankrupt, and the glasshouse was closed down.

As well as the cut articles, visitors could see a selection of pieces with engraved decoration, in which the unpolished shallow cutting contrasted with the shining untouched areas. The London dealer, Joseph George Green, displayed examples that received high praise at the time, the *Art-Journal* stating: 'we scarcely ever remember to have seen glass more exquisitely engraved than in these specimens'. In the *Official Catalogue* were brief entries referring to Green's 'Etruscan shape jugs', and to decoration in the Greek and Francis I styles, both of which were among the many revivals then in favour. The 'Neptune Jug', so-called because of the sea-god's appearance on it, is representative of the best work of the day. Its shaping is equally typical, the high-shouldered body allowing ample space for the broad band of the principal ornamentation. Other jugs of the same date have a comparable appearance, with a trefoil mouth, tall handle and flat circular foot, designated 'Etruscan shape' by their makers and based on the Classical *oenochoë*.

Green's display included: 'Suspending ormolu chandelier, in Elizabethan style, fitted with glass, silvered by Varnish & Co's patent.' The patent mentioned was that of Edward Varnish and F. Hale Thompson, taken out in 1849, relating to a process for making vessels with double walls within which the surfaces were silvered. The silvering was sealed-in, so that tarnishing could not occur. The articles could be left plain, engraved, or cased with one or more colours and then cut through to reveal the mirror-like body (Plates 10 and 11).

Varnish's had their own display, with examples of the patent glass in green, blue and ruby, most of which were said at the time to have been manufactured for them by Powell's of Whitefriars. They were reported on at the time, with a mention of some of the more ambitious pieces: 'Specimens of the beautiful silvered glass lately become so fashionable, and which have formed so ornamental a feature at various public banquets were exhibited by Messrs. Varnish, of Berners-street. The silvered goblets were already familiar to the public, but there were various other articles, such as a chess-table, goblets, curtain-poles, &c., which showed the great adaptability of the material to ornamental purposes.'

Another writer contributed the information that the silvering was performed with a mixture of silver and grape sugar (glucose), but he was less than complimentary about the result: 'The effect, however, is garish, and the articles appear as if made of looking-glass, rather than of silver-plate, which they are intended to represent.' Nevertheless, E. Varnish & Co. were awarded a Prize Medal at the exhibition.

Both Osler's and Lloyd & Summerfield's showed matt-surfaced glass busts, the latter firm including the Queen and her Consort as well as what were described as 'glass medallion busts' of the Duke of Wellington and Sir Robert Peel. These last were presumably moulded cameos or intaglios of the type hand-cut at an earlier date by Dominick Bimann at Prague. The Osler busts also included the Royal couple (Plate 5) and in addition Shakespeare, Milton, Scott and Peel. A note in the *Catalogue* added that their effect 'is pleasant, and would seem to indicate that larger works might with propriety be undertaken of the same kind and material'. The writer concluded with a recommendation that such objects might prove superior to marble for statues and what he termed 'monumental erections'.

To give glass a dull surface was a departure from earlier practice, when makers had always sought a shining finish. Then, in the way that fashions suddenly come and go, a change occurred in the mid-nineteenth century when the public acquired a liking for matt glassware. It became especially popular in the case of the opal glass, which was made in both England and Bohemia in the wake of the French innovation. The soft colourings of the originals were copied, but were invariably garish in comparison, and a touch of gilding was used to compensate for the absence of gilt-metal mounts. Many opal glass articles were made in combinations of two colours: white and green and white and blue being the most common. A proportion of examples had curled about them a glass rod fashioned into a small but realistic-looking snake, sometimes as a handle and in other instances as an ornament. More ambitious opal articles included tall vases, usually in pairs, carefully painted with flowers (Plate 12). Cheaper varieties were smaller in size and often decorated with engraved patterns in the same manner as pottery of the day.

Shapes of mid-century articles varied as at all times, but it is noticeable that the earlier pear-shaped decanter was supplanted by a successor resembling an onion in silhouette. It was sometimes given a low foot, but was equally often footless, with a stopper conforming to the general rotundity.

Apsley Pellatt & Co., owned by Apsley Pellatt the younger, exhibited not only finished goods, but a display of different types of glass, models of furnaces, tools and other items which were explained in an illustrated catalogue of their own. The wares shown included some of Pellatt's patented cameos, named 'Crystallo-ceramies', and known alternatively as 'Cameo-incrustations' or 'sulphides'. They had been devised at the turn of the century by a Frenchman, and took the form of small cameos skilfully enclosed within clear glass so that they acquired an attractive silvery appearance. The articles so treated were further enhanced with cutting to frame and back the cameos.

The English patentee drew attention to the vital importance of balancing the properties of the glass and the porcelain composition of which the cameos were made, or failure would certainly result. He wrote also: 'The figure intended for incrustation must be made of materials that will require a higher degree of heat for their fusion than the glass within which it is to be incrusted; these are china-clay and super-silicate of potash, ground and mixed in such proportions as upon experiment harmonize with the density of the Glass.' Some of the cameos were made for the purpose by Ridgway's of Staffordshire, well known as manufacturers of conventional pottery and porcelain.

Pellatt had begun marketing these novelties soon after he was granted a patent in 1819, and two years later published a book describing and illustrating examples of the cameos embellishing all kinds of articles, the subjects ranging from George IV to the Badge of the Order of the Garter and from Shakespeare to Napoleon. In a later book Apsley Pellatt described how he had used the cameos during the preceding quarter-century: '... ornaments of any description, and landscapes of any variety of colour may be introduced into the glass. ... Specimens of these incrustations have been exhibited not only in decanters and wine-glasses, but in lamps, girandoles, chimney ornaments, plates and smelling bottles. Busts and statues on a small scale to support lamps and clocks and masks after the antique, have been introduced with an admirable effect.'

An adaptation of the process was for the preservation of inscriptions, which were enamelled on a suitable material and then enclosed within a protective coating of clear glass. Examples were used in the 1840s to record building operations that took place at the Tower of London, Windsor Castle and elsewhere. The specimen in Plate 3 was used to record the laying of the foundation stone of the Royal Exchange on 17 January 1842, when a new building was started to replace one burnt down in 1838. The plaque is lettered to record the essential details of the occasion, with the name of the architect concerned, William Tite, at the bottom left, and on the right the words 'Apsley Pellatt, Incrustator'.

Pellatt used the process between about 1820 and 1860. The method of manufacture was complex and unsuitable for large-scale production, but judging by the number of surviving examples there must have been a steady demand. The cameos were also made by a few other firms from the mid-century onwards, and among them was John Ford's Edinburgh glassworks. Predictably, the head of Robert Burns decorated some of the latter's output, but more widely acclaimed personages, such as the Duke of Wellington, were included (Plate 19).

Pellatt's 1851 exhibits comprised not only a selection of his cameo-incrustations, but what was described as 'Anglo-Venetian gilt and

1. Epergne ornamented with cutting. Made by John Ford's Holyrood Flint Glass Works, Edinburgh, to commemorate the accession of Queen Victoria in 1837. Height: 99 cm. *City of Edinburgh Museums and Galleries.*

2. Goblet engraved with barley ears and other ornament and dated SEP[R]. 1837. Height: 19·6 cm. *Torre Abbey Museum, Torquay, Devon.*

3. Plaque commemorating the laying by Queen Victoria of the first stone of the Royal Exchange, London, in 1842. Signed APSLEY PELLATT, GLASS INCRUSTATOR. 26 x 20·6 cm. *Victoria and Albert Museum.*

4. Decanter and stopper cut with shaped panels. About 1845. Height: 31·8 cm. *Victoria and Albert Museum.*

5. Portrait bust of Queen Victoria in moulded glass with a matt surface, marked PUBLISHED BY F. & C. OSLER, 44 OXFORD ST. LONDON. MAY 1ST. 1845. Height: 24·7 cm. *Victoria and Albert Museum.*

6. Carafe painted in colours with water plants. Designed by Richard Redgrave, R.A. for Summerly's Art Manufactures and made by J. F. Christy, Stangate Glass Works, Lambeth, 1847. Height: 26 cm. *Victoria and Albert Museum.*

7. Water jug painted in colours with water-lilies, made by W. H., B. & J. Richardson of Stourbridge, 1848. Marked RICHARDSON'S VITRIFIED, the latter referring to the fact that the decoration was in fired enamels. Height: 23·5 cm. *Victoria and Albert Museum.*

8. Group of examples of Venetian-style glass shown by Bacchus & Sons, Birmingham, at the Great Exhibition, 1851, reproduced from a woodcut in the *Official Catalogue*. The glass in the right foreground is illustrated in Plate 9.

9. Wine-glass in the Venetian style, the bowl engraved and the stem enclosing pink, white and blue threads, made by Bacchus & Sons, Birmingham, 1851. See Plate 8. Height: 12·2 cm. *Victoria and Albert Museum*.

10. Goblet, double-walled and internally silvered, marked E. VARNISH & CO PATENT LONDON, about 1850. Height: 17·8 cm. *Sotheby's Belgravia.*

11. Pair of candlesticks of double-walled clear glass, internally silvered, overlaid with green and cut, about 1850. Marked E. VARNISH & CO PATENT LONDON. Height: 28·9 cm. *Sotheby's Belgravia.*

12. Pair of vases of pale ruby glass overlaid with opaque white, painted in colours with bouquets and decorated with gilding. About 1850. Height: 43 cm. *Christie's*.

13. Bottle of ruby glass mounted as a ewer, the silver mounts by Charles T. and George Fox, London, 1851. Height: 29·8 cm. *Bearne's Torquay*.

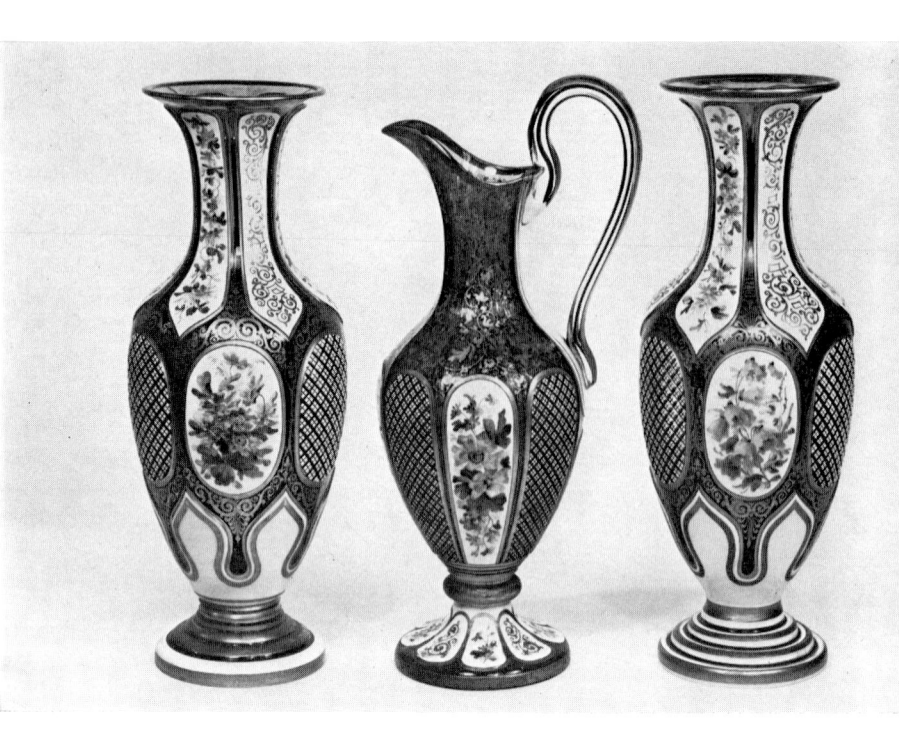

14. Pair of vases and a ewer of ruby glass overlaid with opaque white painted in colours, cut and gilt, attributed to Bacchus & Sons, Birmingham, about 1850. Heights: 35·5 and 36 cm. *Christie's*.

15. Pair of vases of cream-coloured glass painted with Grecian figures within key-fret borders, attributed to Richardson's of Stourbridge, about 1850. Height: 25.6 cm. *Sotheby's Belgravia*.

16. Pair of two-handled vases of clear glass painted in red enamel and gilt, attributed to Richardson's of Stourbridge, about 1850. Height: 26·3 cm. *Victoria and Albert Museum.*

17. Vase of opaque white glass decorated in dark brown with a painted and transfer-printed scene of Bellerophon mounted on Pegasus attacking the Chimæra. Marked GEO. BACCHUS & SONS VITRIFIED ENAMEL COLOURS, about 1850. Height: 35·2 cm. *Victoria and Albert Museum.*

18. Jug of matt-surfaced white opaline glass painted in sepia with the Finding of Moses, made by Richardson's of Stourbridge in about 1850. Height: 22·8 cm. *Victoria and Albert Museum.*

19. Scent bottle inset with a cameo-incrustation showing the head of Arthur, Duke of Wellington (1769–1852), the stopper with a horse and foal in a blue border. Made by Ford's Holyrood Flint Glass Works, Edinburgh, about 1850. Height: 12·7 cm. *City of Edinburgh Museums and Galleries.*

20. Carafe engraved with vine leaves and grapes, the neck rings cut with facets. About 1855. Height: 13 cm.

21. Scent Bottles: (top) in green opaline glass and (bottom) in clear glass overlaid with dark green and cut. About 1850–60. Lengths: 12·2 and 10·2 cm.

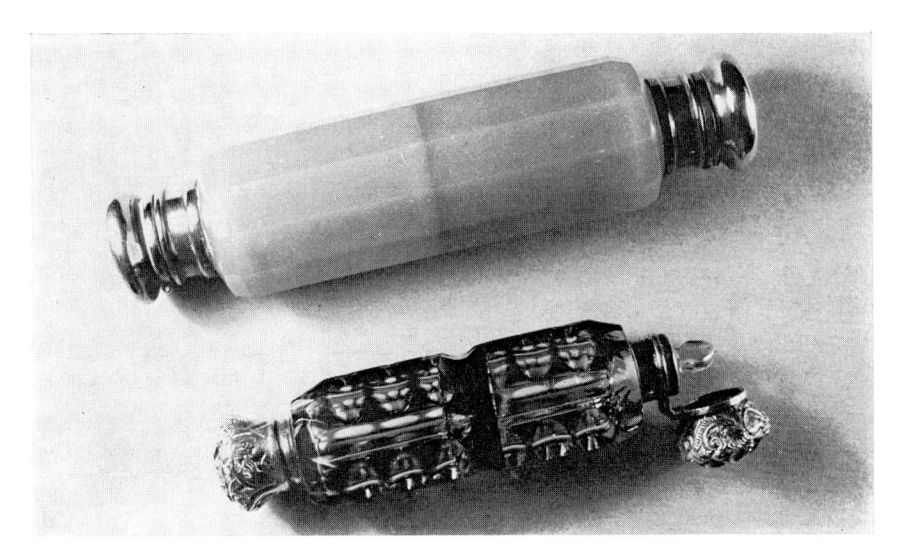

22. Pair of lustres of clear glass decorated with cutting and hung with cut drops, about 1860. Height: 25·7 cm. *Sotheby's Belgravia.*

23. Lustre of ruby glass overlaid with opaque white painted in colours and gilt, and hung with buttons and drops. About 1860. Height: 21·5 cm.

24. Claret jug engraved with a view of the Alexandra Palace, London, and inscribed with a record of its presentation to Sir Sillis John Gibbons, Lord Mayor of London, in 1872. Engraved by F. Eisert. Height: 38·2 cm. *Victoria and Albert Museum.*

25. Amphora of 'Early Italian design', the decoration engraved, designed by F. W. Moody and made by Apsley Pellatt & Co., London, about 1860. The tripod stand silver-plated. Height of amphora: 29·2 cm. *Victoria and Albert Museum.*

frosted glass'. A woodcut illustration shows that it embodied little enough of Venice; a series of dishes on tall stems, wine glasses, a decanter, a carafe and tumbler, a claret jug and a sugar basin with cream jug, all apparently elaborately cut in the fashionable manner. The frosted pieces certainly owed their origin to Murano, although they would be more immediately recognized today if termed 'ice-glass'. This has a surface with the appearance of crushed ice, and its manufacture was the revival of a technique practised in the sixteenth century. Pellatt pointed out with pride that he was the first to make it in modern times, for it had become a lost art and neither the French nor the Bohemians had re-discovered the secret.

It has been suggested with good reason that the general revival of ice-glass and other techniques was due to the keen interest in the history of glass-making shown by Apsley Pellatt. In his *Curiosities of Glassmaking*, published in 1849, he described some of the methods employed by the early craftsmen at Murano, although it is possible that he did not have a very clear idea of the appearance of genuine pieces. He and his fellow manufacturers were soon to have increasing opportunities of studying a good number of specimens of the art of their overseas forerunners.

In 1840 Christie's sold by auction in London a collection of glass belonging to Lady Mary Bagot, among which were some Venetian pieces. They included a *latticinio* salver and a goblet in what was catalogued as 'frostwork', which realized £27 6s. and £15, respectively, and a tall *latticinio* glass that brought £19 15s. These prices were considerably higher than would have been expected in preceding years, and must have caused something of a sensation in days when such antiques were ignored by most and collected by only a small number of people.

A few years later, in 1847, the heirs of a Frenchman named Debruge-Duménil, a Far Eastern merchant who had amassed a large and important collection of objects of art, had his acquisitions catalogued by the foremost authority of the day, Jules Labarte. Then, in 1850, a part of the collection was offered for sale by auction in Paris, with the Venetian glass forming a proportion of the 2,000-odd lots. There were 180 lots of the glass, listed in groups according to type and covering a dozen pages of the sale-catalogue, which sold for an average of £10 a specimen.

Also in 1850, an exhibition was organized in London by the Society of Arts. It was devoted to 'works of Ancient and Medieval Art', and the owners of such objects, who were then only infrequently approached to borrow their possessions, willingly lent them for the purpose. The display was successful in attracting the public, while the Venetian glass and other exhibits were widely commented on in the press.

Thus, by the time that the Great Exhibition opened its doors, Venetian glass, which had been eclipsed since the seventeenth century when George Ravenscroft's wares drove it from the English market, was again becoming known. Soon, the movement in its favour received further encouragement by the formation of the Museum of Ornamental Art, forerunner of the Victoria and Albert Museum, then occupying part of Marlborough House, St James's.

The museum was commenced as a result of the success of the Great Exhibition, when a committee was appointed and given a Parliamentary grant of £5,000 with which to purchase suitable objects for 'the formation of a Museum of Manufactures of a high order of excellence of Design, or rare skill in Workmanship . . .'. As regards glass, the dispersal of the big collection of works of art formed by Ralph Bernal, sold by auction in 1853, proved providential. In a catalogue of the new museum issued three years later there were then seventy-four pieces of glass, of which no fewer than sixty-one were listed as Venetian, and thirty-five of these had come from the Bernal dispersal. Prices at the auction ranged from as low as £1 up to £30 a lot, with the highest in that section of the sale being £54 given by Baron Gustave de Rothschild for what was catalogued as 'a fine large flat tazza, on stem, enamelled with foliage and arabesques, partly gilt'.

As well as Pellatt, Bacchus & Sons attempted to translate the Venetian sixteenth- and seventeenth-century styles into nineteenth-century English, and in 1851 exhibited some champagnes with colour-twist stems. The stems were twisted into one or more loops midway, a feature that was arguably decorative. The glasses were illustrated in the *Catalogue* as 'Venetian', along with a tall glass of equally bizarre appearance. While the workmanship could not be faulted, as in the case of so much else to be seen in the Crystal Palace, the glasses were impractical and could be justified only as examples of their maker's virtuosity. None the less, against all odds, at least one of the loop-stemmed glasses has been preserved and can be seen in the Victoria and Albert Museum (Plate 9).

The craftsmen of the time did their best to imitate Venetian models, but they were handicapped in their efforts by the properties peculiar to English flint glass. The originals were made from a metal incorporating soda as the principal flux, which gave it the quality of cooling more slowly in comparison with the English. This allowed the Venetians time during which to manipulate the material and form it into complex shapes without frequent re-heating, whereas the contrasting quick-cooling flint glass did not respond easily to the same treatment.

Furthermore, Venice is credited with being the place where one of the revivals of ancient Roman glass-making techniques originated; one which played a small and barely noticed role at Hyde Park in 1851. Among the foreign exhibitors was Pietro Bigaglia who had exhibited a selection of millefiori glass paperweights in Vienna six years before. In 1849, Apsley Pellatt illustrated one in colour in his book *Curiosities of Glass Making*, giving it the caption 'Venetian Ball', and in the accompanying text described methods of making the so-called 'scrambled' and 'patterned millefiori' varieties. The exhibition in Vienna was visited by a Frenchman who reported on what he had seen in the Austrian capital after he had returned to Paris. As a result, improved versions were put on the market in 1846 by French glass-makers, and achieved immediate success. At or about the same date comparable weights to the French ones were also being made in Bohemia.

In order that they might judge the merits of the thousands of items shown at the Great Exhibition, the organizers divided and sub-divided them into convenient categories. Glass was Class XXIV, of which subsection 5 of section F comprised: 'Glass Mosaic, Millefiori, Aventurine, and Venetian Glass Weights, &c.' So, despite the fact that French-made paperweights had been produced for some five years, the name of Venice still clung to them. This may well have been because the long-standing fame of Venetian wares was a superior sales feature, but also the traditional English wariness of France, alerted by the recent and continuing political troubles in that country, might have made many Englishmen somewhat reluctant to knowingly buy French goods.

The report of the jury that dealt with glass noted, after mentioning coloured articles: '... likewise the *mille fiori* style of work, adopted for making presse papiers and other ornaments, and sold by hundreds of thousands, which by the extent of the trade, have become a very important branch of manufacture.' It is perhaps surprising, therefore, that paperweights are not actually specified as being included among the exhibits of the various makers, and it must be assumed that the abbreviation 'etc.', which appears frequently at the end of lists of goods, effectively conceals them. On the other hand, the principal French glassworks, because of the troubles then besetting the country, were not represented comprehensively in London, but there is evidence that the Clichy firm certainly had paperweights on display. The other known French makers of them, Baccarat and St Louis, sent neither weights nor anything else.

Whether any English-made paperweights were exhibited in 1851 remains a debatable point, but there is no doubt that they were being made at about that date. The 1848 exhibition held in the capital by the Society of Arts included some examples, about which a report on the display under the heading 'Glass Paper Weights' noted those made by Bacchus of Birmingham. The same firm co-operated also in an exhibition of Manufactures and Arts held in Birmingham in 1849, where they showed a variety of goods which included 'Letter weights': an alternative term for the one that duly attained popularity and endured. Rice Harris & Son also exhibited at the 1849 Birmingham show, although there is no record that paperweights were included in their display. It is known, however, that they were making them at about that date, and a few have been recorded with the strongest evidence for attributing them to the firm. They are of millefiori pattern with the addition of a cane lettered I G W, which it has been very reasonably suggested stands for Islington Glass Works.

The English paperweights proved unable to compete with those from France; from identified examples it seems that they were less novel in pattern and distinctive in finish, and they possibly could not be sold as cheaply. The French had quickly organized their production and were able to turn them out in quantity and therefore at lower cost. The imported ones doubtless provided the bulk of the alleged 'hundreds of thousands' said to have been on the market. It is not known exactly when English production of the weights ceased, but from the paucity of surviving examples their output was probably small and confined to a period of no more than a few years. Whether firms other than Rice Harris and Bacchus made them then is also a moot point.

Not all the glassware sold in the 1850s was ornate and costly; makers and dealers were keen to sell their better and more expensive goods, so commonplace varieties seldom received attention. In addition to their productions noted above, Rice Harris & Son displayed in 1851: 'Pressed and moulded glass tumblers, goblets, wines, sugar-basins, butter-coolers, salt-cellars, honey-pots, door-knobs, &c.'

Reliable comments on the availability of cheap glassware were printed by Henry Mayhew in his book *London Labour and the London Poor*, which was published between 1851 and 1864. He noted that street-sellers of second-hand glass were seldom to be seen in the capital at the date of writing: 'before glass and crockery, but more especially glass, became so low-priced when new, the secondhand glass-man was one of the most prosperous of the secondhand traders; he is now the reverse . . .'. An ex-seller told Mayhew that it had once been a profitable trade, he made 15s. to £1 a week at it, but that was in the past and it was so long ago that he could not recall the exact year. Mayhew referred to the popularity of pressed glass, which he referred to as 'cast', and its effect on what was to be seen in the streets: 'At the period before cast-glass was so common, and, indeed, subsequently, until glass became cheap, it was not unusual to see at the secondhand stalls, rich cut-glass vessels which had been broken and cemented, for sale at a low figure, the glass-man being often a mender.'

One of the features of the Victorian home that is renowned as especially typical would seem to have begun its lengthy enjoyment of popularity at about the time of the Great Exhibition. This is the glass lustre, a cross between a vase and a candlestick but without any real function except to be ornamental (Plate 23). The lustre varied in design over the years, its decoration ranging from cutting to casing with painting and gilding or, in its cheaper versions, to harshly tinted opal or coloured glass. At all times and whatever its quality it was mandatory that it should bear a fringe of cut prisms and drops suspended from the rim. Lustres were made and sold in pairs, and judging by the immense numbers that have come on the market from the later 1940s onwards, there could not have been many British homes that did not once boast their quota.

Glass also played a part in the mid-century, less predictably than elsewhere, in clothing and saddlery. Buttons were made of glass, moulded with holes ready for stitching, or with a single larger hole through which a metal shank could be riveted in place. The buttons were formed by what was termed 'pinching', using a pliers-like tool for the purpose. This had the shape and ornament of the button cut into its jaws in intaglio, so that a small piece of molten glass could be squeezed between them to be easily and quickly completed. Another kind was somewhat more complex in its making, requiring a sheet of clear or coloured glass to be coated with lead foil and then cut into pieces of the required size and shape. These were heated to melt the lead, and prepared pieces of tinned metal, already complete with shanks, were soldered to the lead-back glass. Each button was then finished by being cut to its final shape and given a decorative cut pattern on the front.

The foregoing were manufactured by Neal & Tonks of Birmingham, and doubtless also by others there and elsewhere. The same firm also supplied glass shirt studs, and what they described as 'coat loops in fancy glass'. No further description of the latter appears to exist, and it may be surmised whether a coat loop was perhaps a fastening in the form of some kind of toggle. Neal & Tonks's other products included 'horses' bridle rosettes in fancy cut glass', which must have had a very smart appearance as well as a high rate of breakage.

3
The influence of Venice

The early 1860s were dominated by another exhibition which, like that of the preceding decade, provides important information about the glassware of the day. The 1862 International Exhibition was also organized by the Society of Arts, whose original intention had been to hold it exactly ten years after the earlier display, but the outbreak of the Franco-Prussian war in 1859 caused postponement of the scheme. The war surprised everyone by its brevity, a delay of no more than a single year was necessitated and 1862 became the revised target.

Optimistically it was concluded that without any doubt the tremendous success of the 1851 exhibition could not fail to be repeated, but while the sequel was by no means a failure it made a much slighter impact than the other. The Prince Consort, who was again at the head of the Commissioners, became unwell while attending one of their meetings, and before the end of 1861 died of what was at first thought to be influenza. In fact, it was typhoid fever. The event shocked the entire nation to such a degree that interest in the projected exhibition noticeably diminished.

However, preparations had begun and were continued. A site was selected in Kensington, not far distant from where the Crystal Palace had stood, and Captain Francis Fowke, of the Royal Engineers, designed a building for the purpose. This did not satisfy everyone, and there followed a long and bitter controversy as to why he had been chosen and whether the building would prove to be suitable. In the end, the exhibition was opened and between 1 May and 15 November 6,211,103 visitors paid the sum of £89,248 for admission. Unlike the earlier occasion, income and expenditure exactly balanced each other, so that neither profit nor loss resulted: a fact that provided further fuel for critical comment.

The building was much less like a conservatory than the Crystal Palace, but nevertheless incorporated 200,000 panes of glass in its construction. Among the exhibitors of glass were some who had shown their wares on the previous occasion: Green and Apsley Pellatt of London, and Osler of Birmingham, while newcomers included Dobson & Pearce of London, and Miller & Co. of Edinburgh. The latter was a decorating concern owned by a Bohemian immigrant and his son who had changed their surname from Müller. They were deft engravers, said to specialize in depicting birds and other natural subjects and obtained their blank glassware from Ford's Holyrood works.

One of the articles shown by Dobson & Pearce, who had premises in St James's Street, was illustrated in the *Art-Journal* catalogue of the exhibition and is shown in Plate 26. Named the 'Ailsa Jug', it was doubtless intended more as a cabinet piece than as a container for claret, and was priced at fifty guineas (£52.50). The body of the jug is engraved with cornucopias of fruit and flowers and with swans amid bullrushes issuing from tiered fountains; the whole distinctly reminiscent of the famous *grotesques* designed by Raphael for the *loggia* of the Vatican. The productions of the makers received high praise from some of the contributors to the *Art-Journal*, one of whom rhapsodized about 'the beautiful forms produced by Dobson and Pearce, with ornamentation which passes from Art-industry into high-class engraving', while another, perhaps stirred to some degree by patriotic emotions, noted that 'there are many excellent exhibitors of Table Glass, who have all, foreigners included, willingly admitted that none of their exhibits compete with those of the eminent firm in St. James's Street'.

Articles in daily use in the home varied little, if at all, from those available at earlier dates. The catalogue of an on-the-premises auction at a London house in December 1866 lists what would have been the average contents of a Mayfair pantry. The glassware included: waterjugs; goblets; claret jugs; decanters; sugar vases; 'finger glasses', better-known as finger-bowls; water-bottles and tumblers; 'flat bowl champagne glasses'; glasses for ale, hock (these last in green glass), claret, rum and liqueur; 'lipped wine coolers', which were similar to finger-bowls but with lips to hold the stems of wine glasses; celery vases; 'soda water glasses'; dishes, ice plates; and 'a glass dessert service, 30 pieces'. The latter item was disposed of at the sale for 19s. (95p).

A few years before, in 1862, Osler's had advertised: 'Glass Dessert Services, for 12 persons, from £2', and 'Glass Dinner Services, for 12 persons, from £7 15s.' The last-named would hardly have been a practical proposition, at least for a hot meal, as only during the present century have suitable metals for the purpose been developed commercially. Possibly such a dinner service was intended for use in the summer with salads, but in any case the domestic servants of the day, and later, would have played havoc with such breakables, which is why all traces have apparently vanished.

The shapes of articles current in 1862 varied in some instances from those of a decade before, but many had scarcely changed at all. Some of the decanters were of the onion shape noticed earlier, while others had an upright oval outline that was shared by many vases and jugs. A proportion continued to be variations of the old Grecian *oenochoë*, the decoration sometimes including such appropriate motifs as the anthemion and key pattern, but these were also likely to be found on shapes owing nothing to classical prototypes. Delicate engraving and heavy cutting vied with one another for popularity, and sometimes appeared in conjunction on the same article. The stems of wine glasses were as varied as ever: plain or cut in facets, but sometimes in the form of rope-like twisted rods distantly echoing Venice.

A fresh source of inspiration was the common fern. The preceding decade had seen a slowly-increasing interest in its cultivation, with articles in magazines as well as complete books devoted to the introduction of these docile examples of wild Nature into the drawing-room. The curving, delicate fronds were well adapted for use as ornamental motifs, and by the early 1860s were appearing on glass tumblers, wine glasses, jugs, and so forth; their introduction allegedly being due to the Millers' Edinburgh workshop. Ferns continued to provide inspiration for decorators during the succeeding twenty years and more, when what a writer termed 'a world of moisture and shadows' ceased to fascinate.

In contrast to what had occurred in 1851, the striking feature about the exhibitors of glass in 1862 was that none from Stourbridge took part. From this it may be inferred that the Midlanders were prospering sufficiently without the considerable extra effort demanded in making wares suitable for display. Free of Government interference, the manufacturers could concentrate on normal production, making improvements as they saw fit, and reap the full benefit of their enterprise.

Some of the names of families still active today in the Stourbridge area were not unknown over a century ago, and successive generations have maintained the reputation of the industry there. In the same way as Staffordshire is synonymous with pottery and porcelain, so the nearby area about the river Stour is renowned for glass. The practical goods made by the early settlers from Lorraine, sheet and bottle glass, were gradually widened to include drinking vessels and ornamental articles, so that by the mid-nineteenth century it was these last that formed the greater proportion of the output. The success achieved by the makers from the area at the 1851 exhibition confirmed that Stourbridge could hold its own against the rest of England, and this it continued to do.

There was much interchanging of partners between firms over the years, each man taking his own ideas with him and accounting for the difficulty, or impossibility, of identifying the precise origins of most of the wares. Competition was intense, and as soon as a particular pattern or style was found to be saleable it would be copied as closely as possible. Equally, patterns were kept in production for as long as there was any demand for them, so that there are often only very slight differences observable between articles ranging in date over a period of as much as a half-century.

The Richardson brothers, Benjamin, William Haden and Jonathan, were particularly active in exploiting new ideas. Benjamin earned for himself the reputation of being an 'ingenious gentleman', and by the date of his death, 30 November 1887, at the age of 85, was referred to as 'the father of the trade'. The brothers traded as W. H., B. & J. Richardson from 1829 to 1852, then the firm was listed under the name of Benjamin alone until 1862 when it became Hodgetts, Richardson & Pargeter. Benjamin Richardson gained a reputation for devising fresh methods of decorating, and at an early date showed an interest in etching glass. The process was in occasional use by the mid-century, and in 1857 Richardson was granted a patent for his own method of applying the acid. In the ensuing decades the process was employed on an increasing scale.

A partner of Benjamin Richardson in the 1820s was Thomas Webb, Sr, who later, with various others, set up in business and contributed to the rise of Stourbridge. Both Benjamin Richardson and William Greathead, of David, Greathead & Green, had begun their careers at the glassworks of Thomas Hawkes & Co., of Dudley, a few miles distant from Stourbridge. Hawkes supplied a gilt-decorated dessert service to the Corporation of the City of London for use on Queen

Victoria's visit to the Guildhall in 1837, and a few years later it was stated that 'their articles in opal, turquoy, and gold enamel stand unrivalled'. The company ceased trading in the mid-1840s, and their employees doubtless quickly found work at other establishments in the area.

Many other firms also came and went, partners were exchanged, and in some instances marriages resulted in the uniting of families and firms. On the other hand, there were numerous small concerns that remain completely unrecorded; they existed to make money to pay their bills and with no eye to such an intangible thing as future fame. These cribs, which had always been active, although keeping themselves away from the prying eyes of the duty-collectors, expanded in number after 1845. They proved a bane to both the larger manufacturers and to the unions which were trying to organize the craftsmen. 'The National Flint Glass Makers' Friendly Society of Great Britain and Ireland' represented blowers and other workers at the furnace, while 'The United Flint Glass Cutters' took care of the interests of those at the wheel.

For many years the societies were far from strong, the Makers' reporting in 1854 that the year had seen an improvement in membership and announcing that the Stourbridge area then boasted thirty-two. As with other unions, those in the glass industry strove to limit the number of apprentices, using every means at their disposal to gain increases in pay and additional privileges. At the same time, they endeavoured to safeguard the health of their members, who were at risk in using many of the processes then in use. They did their best to ensure that employers took all possible precautions.

There was intermittent sparring between the employers and Society members, with the former sometimes circularizing their fellows whenever drastic action was taken or might appear worthwhile. In October 1858, one of the firms sent round a notice listing their dissident workers with the introductory words: 'The following men having formed a Combination to stop our Glass Works, and dictate their own rules, have all been discharged by us; and we should be obliged by your not employing them, and feel sure it is in the interest of the Glass Trade to support us. Our Glass Cutters are all men unconnected with the Union, and we mean to adopt the same course with the Glass Makers.'

The manufacturers had their own organization, 'The Flint Glass

Trade', but both sides of the industry included those on either side who preferred to remain outside such bodies. They were referred to at the time as 'black rats' or 'traitors', and in 1850 Powell's of Whitefriars were censured by their brother makers. Powell's had issued a list of prices lower than those prevailing, at which 'extreme surprise and regret' were expressed and the opinion given 'that the course pursued will have the most disastrous consequences'. Attempts continued to be made during the course of the century to band all eligible persons and groups into their appropriate association, but there were always some who remained aloof for one reason or another.

The biggest makers at Stourbridge and elsewhere had their own cutting shops, but there were also cutters who worked as independent concerns. They would buy their requirements from one or many manufacturers and arrange the marketing of the finished goods as they pleased. The independent shop was sometimes a simple backyard concern working in conjunction with a crib, the completed article often lacking the distinction of design and good finish of the company-made piece, but invariably being sold more cheaply than the latter. The more important and larger cutting-shops were as well set up as the glass-houses, and no doubt the fact that each branch of the trade had its separate union encouraged them to remain distinct.

Like any other industry, that of glass manufacture was well organized, with a pride in its productions and a high level of skill in its various branches. In particular, cutting, which had featured on English glass continuously since the second half of the eighteenth century, had become a traditional mode of ornamentation and there seemed to be no reason why it should cease to be in demand in ever-increasing quantities. Such a calculation disregarded any possibility of a change in taste, and although this only affected a proportion of buyers it gradually took place.

From the late 1840s there had been a ground-swell of opinion directed against decorated glassware, particularly pieces that were cut or engraved. The Jury reporting on the glass shown at the Great Exhibition wrote of the misapplied ingenuity of manufacturers who attempted to imitate porcelain or japanned tin, of the tendency to make thick-walled and clumsy vessels covered with ornament that obscured the contents, and of cutting carried to extremes 'tending to vulgarize, as far as possible, the simple and beautiful material'.

The censure was amplified by the respected pen of the art critic, John Ruskin. His book, *The Stones of Venice*, dealt with the architecture of the city and was published in 1853. The second of the three volumes into which the work was divided included twelve appendixes, the final one being headed 'Modern Painting on Glass'. In it, the writer analysed the characters of the material:

These are two, namely, its DUCTILITY when heated, and TRANSPARENCY when cold, both nearly perfect. In its employment for vessels, we ought always to exhibit its ductility, and in its employment for windows its transparency. All work in glass is bad which does not, with loud voice, proclaim one or other of these great qualities.

Consequently, *all cut glass* is barbarous: for the cutting conceals its ductility, and confuses it with crystal [rock-crystal]. Also, all very neat, finished, and perfect form in glass is barbarous: for this fails in proclaiming another of its great virtues; namely, the ease with which its light substance can be moulded or blown into any form, so long as perfect accuracy be not required. In metal, which, even when heated enough to be thoroughly malleable, retains yet such weight and consistency as render it susceptible of the finest handling and retention of the most delicate form, great precision of workmanship is admissible; but in glass, which when once softened must be blown or moulded, not hammered, and which is liable to lose, by contraction or subsidence, the finest of the forms given to it, no delicate outlines are to be attempted, but only such fantastic and fickle grace as the mind of the workman can conceive and execute on the instant. The more wild, extravagant, and grotesque in their gracefulness the forms are, the better. No material is so adapted for giving full play to the imagination, but it must not be wrought with refinement or painfulness, still less with costliness. For as in gratitude we are to proclaim its virtues, so in all honesty we are to confess its imperfections; and while we triumphantly set forth its transparency, we are also frankly to admit its fragility, and therefore not to waste much time upon it, nor put any real art into it when intended for daily use. No workman ought ever to spend more than an hour in the making of any glass vessel.

John Ruskin's statement was not only a lengthy one, but it had behind it all the authority of the man who had successfully defended the painter, Turner, against the attacks of critics and public indifference to his merits. No doubt both buyers and makers of glass were scandalized at the final summing-up: 'no workman ought to spend more than an hour in the making of any glass vessel'. Such revolutionary words must have shocked, above all, those who made and dealt in cut and engraved pieces, some of whom handled examples on which not just a single hour but days or weeks had been expended. Most probably, however, the inflammatory words failed to penetrate the walls of the workshops, but were read and eagerly discussed by some of the younger and more thoughtful students of the day.

Among them was William Morris, born in 1834, son of well-to-do parents, who acquired a taste for architecture while at school at Marlborough. Up at Oxford in 1853 he formed a friendship with Edward Burne-Jones, later to become well known as an artist, but at that time, like Morris, interested in taking holy orders. In the end, William Morris returned to the study of architecture and in due course worked in an architect's office. In 1869 he married, and then began building for himself and his wife a house in which every feature of the structure and its contents was specially designed. As a result of the experience he gained from this and despite the fact that the new home proved unhealthy to live in, Morris established a company in London. Its purpose was to undertake wood-carving, stained glass, metalwork, wallpapers, fabrics of many kinds and the decoration of churches.

The infection of Ruskin's ideals was in the air, and when he duly championed the Pre-Raphaelite painters against the storm of abuse aroused by their work, he gained an increased and even more devoted following. The group of painters included in their number Burne-Jones as well as Dante Gabriel Rossetti, the latter also an Oxford friend; later both became business partners of Morris. Looking afresh at the contents of the home embraced not only furniture and fabrics, but also glassware. Functionalism combined with good craftsmanship were the goals to be reached, and later Morris summed up his aims in these words: 'Have nothing in your house that you do not know to be useful or believe to be beautiful'. In due course the influence of Ruskin, by way of Morris, was to be felt. In the meantime, a discerning, but very limited, number of people began to appreciate glassware differing in appearance from that generally available, but other currents of taste were flowing. It was to be a few years yet before any significant changes in style became apparent to the man in the street.

The earlier interest shown in Venetian glass continued during the 1860s. An important loan exhibition held at South Kensington Museum, later the Victoria and Albert, was contributed to by about 500 owners up and down the country. The 9,000 or so exhibits included a section devoted to glass of many countries and periods, the Venetian pieces comprising a number belonging to Felix Slade. He founded the Slade Professorship of Fine Art at Oxford, and following his death in 1866 much of the glass went to the British Museum in accordance with the terms of his will.

The prices of old examples continued to rise, and the number of collectors increased. The sequel to this was renewed activity in Venice, where a number of small glasshouses had continued to supply requirements. Their ranks were swelled in 1864 by Antonio Salviati, who has since been hailed as the man 'to whose successful efforts the modern renaissance of Venetian glass is principally due'. Within two years of establishing his concern, the *Art-Journal* put its readers on their guard: 'It is necessary to warn collectors that many of the modern productions of Salviati are selling as veritable antiques. Those who are not experienced connoisseurs may be easily deceived, for the imitations – rather copies – cannot be at once distinguished from the old. They are as light and as soft to the touch; the semi-transparency has been preserved, the colours are often brilliant, and the designs are, in nearly all instances, after veritable models.'

It would appear that such a warning was required, and in at least one instance was heeded. One of England's keenest collectors, Lady Charlotte Schreiber, who later gave much of her accumulation of china, fans and other objects to the British Museum and the Victoria and Albert Museum, arrived at Venice on 7 June 1869. Under the seventeenth of the month she listed in her Journal the acquisitions she had made during the preceding few days, adding: 'as to the glass, we got Signor Montecchi, the Director of the Salviati Works, to come and give us his opinion of it'. He rejected two 'Amorini vases', but praised some of the other purchases. 'It ended', wrote Lady Charlotte, 'by our rejecting Favenza's [the dealer who had sold them] 2 glass vases with Amorini, for on washing them we found the colouring defective.'

Among others who advocated the merits of Venetian glass was Charles Locke Eastlake, secretary to the Royal Institute of British Architects from 1866 to 1877 and then keeper and secretary of the National Gallery, who published an influential book in 1868 entitled *Hints on Household Taste*. In it he wrote with enthusiasm of the revival of the Venetian ware: 'Dr. Salviati has done his best to procure good designs (some of which have been furnished by Mr. Norman Shaw), and old examples for the men to copy. Last year a large depôt for the table glass, under the management of an English company, aided by the exertions and valuable advice of Mr. A. H. Layard, was opened in St. James's Street; and considering how short a time has elapsed since the first attempt was made, the specimens which have reached England are remarkably good. Here may be seen in rich variety of form and colour, water-bottles, claret jugs, tumblers, wine and liqueur glasses, salt-cellars, preserve jars, flower-stands, tazze, vases, &c., &c., many of them very beautiful in design and all possessing qualities of material which we seek in vain among our native ware.'

Layard had gained an international prominence as a result of his two excavations of the remains of Nineveh and Babylon, undertaken between 1845 and 1852, of which many of the important finds are in the British Museum. He then returned to England, became a Member of Parliament and by 1866 was appointed Under-Secretary for Foreign Affairs and a trustee of the British Museum. In 1878, Layard was knighted and finally retired to live in Venice, where he collected paintings and wrote on the subject of Italian art. He was, therefore, a man whose opinions carried weight, and whose championing of Salviati would have gone a long way towards ensuring the success of his glass in England.

Eastlake, to prove his case, illustrated his words of commendation with a full-page drawing from his own pen, so that his readers could have been in no doubt as to what he had in mind. To hammer home the point further he wrote: 'Of course, the smooth perfection and stereotyped neatness of ordinary English goods are neither aimed at nor found in this ware. But if fair colour, free grace of form, and artistic quality of material, constitute excellence in such manufacture, this is the best modern table glass which has been produced.'

26. 'The Ailsa Jug', of engraved clear glass, shown by Dobson & Pearce at the International Exhibition, London, 1862, when it was described as bearing a 'Raffaellesque ornamental scroll design, fountain, fruit and flowers'. Height: 33 cm. *Sotheby's Belgravia.*

27. Jug of clear glass engraved with a charioteer above a border of key-fret and Vitruvian scroll patterns. Perhaps engraved by John Smith of Leith on a blank from Ford's Edinburgh glasshouse, about 1860. Height: 23·8 cm. *City of Edinburgh Museums and Galleries.*

28. Wine-glass engraved with a seated hound and foliage, perhaps by Miller (or Millar) on a blank from Ford's Edinburgh glasshouse, about 1860. Height: 13·3 cm. *City of Edinburgh Museums and Galleries.*

29. Part of a table service probably designed for William Morris by Philip Webb in 1859. Height of wine-glass (left): 12·7 cm. *Victoria and Albert Museum.*

30. Comport, press-moulded in clear glass, made by Percival Vickers & Co., Ltd., Manchester, who registered the design in 1867. Height: 17·8 cm. *Victoria and Albert Museum.*

31. Fairy lamp for burning oil: numbers of these could be linked together and suspended for outdoor illumination. Diameter: 7 cm.

32. Two-handled celery vase patterned with ferns, the design registered at the Patent Office in 1869 by T. Webb & Sons of Stourbridge. Height: 22·5 cm. *Victoria and Albert Museum.*

33. Goblet engraved with a view of the Town Hall, Manchester, and an inscription recording its presentation to Alderman Heywood, Mayor of the city, in 1877, 'By the Workmen of the Firm of Messrs. Andrew Ker & Co., Prussia Street Flint Glassworks Oldham Road'. Height: 39·6 cm. *City Art Gallery, Manchester.*

34. Water jug with etched decoration of passion flowers, about 1870. Height: 28·5 cm. *Mr. and Mrs. F. C. G. Cary.*

35. Cameo glass showing stages in its manufacture: (left) a Portland vase with the design protected by varnish where the top layer of glass is not to be removed by acid; (centre) a vase with the top layer eaten away where unprotected and the remainder in flat relief; (right) a finished example with a pattern of currants and foliage; and (bottom left) typical carving tools. *Crown Copyright. Science Museum, London.*

36. Vase of claret-coloured and opaque white glass with a cameo of Hebe, signed by George Woodall. Height: 23 cm. *Phillips*.

37. Plaque in spinach-green and opaque white glass with a cameo of a nymph in a crescent moon, by Ludwig Kny. Diameter: 24 cm. *Christie's*.

38. Plaque by George Woodall, 'formerly student of the Stourbridge School of Art, and manufactured by T. Webb & Sons, Stourbridge', about 1884. 5·7 x 11·4 cm. *Victoria and Albert Museum*.

39. Scent bottle of ruby glass carved with a flowering plant and impressed STEVENS & WILLIAMS PATENT ART GLASS STOURBRIDGE, the silver mount hallmarked Birmingham, 1887. Height: 10·4 cm. *Bearnes, Torquay.*

40. Two vases: (left) with a floral design in pink and white on a bright yellow ground, and (right) with poppies in white on a brown ground. Late-nineteenth century. Heights: 12·7 and 10·8 cm. *Bearnes, Torquay.*

41. Bowl of pink glass overlaid with white and patterned with peaches, plums and a pear below the rim of overlapping leaves in yellow. Late-nineteenth century. Diameter: 15·2 cm. *Phillips.*

42. Vase of olive-green overlaid with blue, pink and opaque white and patterned with fruiting peach sprigs. Late nineteenth century. Height: 26·5 cm. *Christie's.*

43. Scent bottles with cameo decoration by H. A. Davies (1860–1942), assistant to George Woodall; the bottles at left and right with silver mounts hallmarked 1889. Lengths (left to right): 8, 14 and 8 cm. *Christie's.*

44. Vase of 'Ivory Cameo' etched and engraved in the Persian taste with shaped panels of birds and foliage, marked THOMAS WEBB & SONS, about 1880. Height: 15·9 cm. *Sotheby's Belgravia.*

45. Basket of clear glass shading to green at the rim and bound with clear threads, about 1880. Height: 19·7 cm.

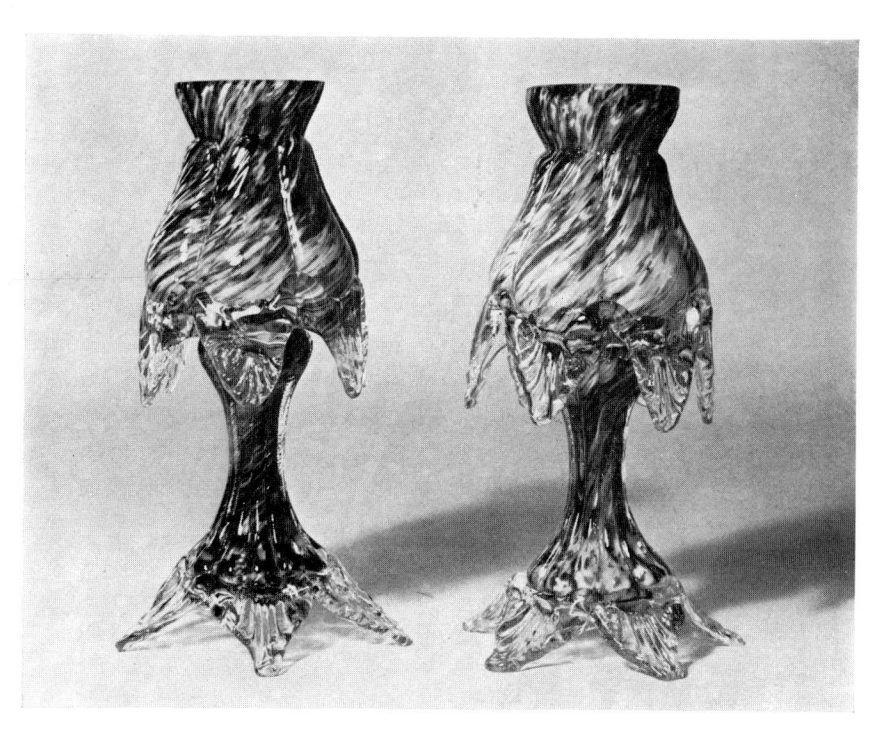

46. Pair of vases of vari-coloured glass overlaid with clear, the feet and central ornaments in the shape of leaves of clear glass and the interior of opaque white. Late-nineteenth century. Height: 17·5 cm.

47. Jar and cover of ruby-coloured glass, the lower part of the jar horizontally ribbed and the cover with a clear glass finial. Late-nineteenth century. Height: 18 cm.

48. Bowl and cover of topaz-coloured glass enclosing swirling white tapes, the leaf-form feet and finial in pale pink. Late-nineteenth century. Height: 16 cm.

49. Pot of opalescent white glass, the lower part spattered in pink, green, red, blue, white and yellow. Late-nineteenth century. Diameter: 8 cm.

Probably unknown to Eastlake, but likely to have been within the ken of John Ruskin, there was already in existence some English-made glassware that fulfilled the ideals of both men. It was a suite of pieces for use at the table, tumblers and other vessels, designed in 1859 for William Morris's newly built house. Webb had made the acquaintance of Morris when they were both working in the same architect's office, and he duly became a partner in Morris's firm of decorative craftsmen: Morris, Marshall, Faulkner & Co. The glass in question has been assumed to be a set of which examples are in the Victoria and Albert Museum. The wine glass illustrated (Plate 29) is notable for the series of horizontal ribs on the bowl; a feature that is to be seen also on the tumblers and finger bowls in the set. The ribs clearly exemplify Morris's desire for practicability, for they are not merely ornamental; they provide a satisfactory grip when the article is in use. The glasses were made by Powell's of Whitefriars, and it was a later member of the firm, Harry J. Powell, who suggested in 1923 that they were the ones supplied some sixty years earlier to William Morris.

Demand for what were then novel articles was probably very slow in building up. The taste of the educated buying public of the sixties was divided, but unevenly in numbers, between traditional English cut and engraved wares and Venetian with manipulated ornament and colouring. Demand for the latter was not filled entirely by imported goods, for the chandelier in Plate 56, which might be mistaken at a glance for one of Venetian origin, was in fact made by Powell's in about 1865. Certainly it was completed prior to 1866, in which year it is recorded as having been acquired by the Victoria and Albert Museum.

In addition to its normal useful and decorative roles, glass played its part in one of the popular hobbies of the day, namely Potichomanie, a simply-contrived method of decorating vases for the home. It was performed by sticking selected small prints on the insides of clear glass vases, and then colouring the unfilled spaces. Very little more than a minimum patience was required, which may explain why the 'art', which seems to have attracted attention in the mid-fifties, was still being practised several years later.

No fewer than four advertisers in the *Illustrated London News* of 18 December 1854 offered their assistance to interested readers. One of them worded his announcement as follows:

POTICHOMANIE. – Mr. Wright begs to call the attention of Ladies to this simple and Fashionable ART, recently introduced from Paris, by which plain glass potiches are converted into beautiful Imitations of India, Sèvres, and other styles of Vases.

Instructions given, together with a set of Materials, for 10s. 6d. By following Mr. Wright's Instructions a considerable saving of materials will be effected. Specimens on view daily from 12 till 4. – 102 Great Russell-street, Bloomsbury.

In the following year, Jabez Barnard of Oxford Street offered his clients a boxed set of a pair of 8-in vases and all the necessary accessories, post free, for 10s. 6d. He stated also that he stocked scented paint 'and every other Article connected with the Art'.

By 1862 the range of motifs available had increased. Messrs Hooman & Maliskeski displayed at the exhibition of that year 'Photographic portraiture for the interior of glass vases, &c.'. Examples of vases and other items ornamented with prints or photographs must once have been numerous, but are now scarce. Time has obliterated the scent from the background colours, which have themselves faded, the carefully-placed pieces of paper have begun to peel away or have fallen off long ago, and most surviving specimens bear little resemblance to what they were like in the past.

One further glass article, commonplace for a century or more, still current in the 1860s and later, but completely superseded in modern times, deserves a mention. It is the fairy lamp, in appearance like a miniature goldfish bowl but serving a very different purpose. The lamps were used for outdoor fêtes and gatherings, at which they were for long the only satisfactory illuminant. Each bowl held oil and a wick, and as many as were required could be linked by means of a string tied round the neck and leading from one bowl to another.

Cecil Torr recorded that 'there were illuminations for Queen Victoria's wedding [10 February 1840]; and the house was decked with night-lights in little globes of coloured glass. Ann put them carefully away, and brought them out in 1887 for the Jubilee'. These, or similar lamps, were employed to light up the transparencies exhibited on such occasions, when private citizens, clubs, businesses and others vied in demonstrating their patriotism and attracting public attention.

The transparencies were made of painted cloth, treated to allow as much light as possible to show through it. The cloth was stretched tightly over a frame, and with the picture or message painted on it had the lamps placed behind. The effect would scarcely be as vivid as that of coloured neon-tubes, but prior to the invention of the latter it must have given considerable pleasure.

4
Etching and Cameo-carving

Industrial success can be measured by the ability of a trade to manufacture ever more cheaply and supply ever more customers, while continuing to make a profit. In the fulfilment of that objective the makers of glassware during the nineteenth century were in the forefront, and continued to increase their output while lowering prices. By the late 1850s it was realized that the old methods of cutting ornament, which were both slow and costly, must be superseded by some other decorative process with an equal appeal to the public.

Richardson's of Stourbridge were experimenting with the use of hydrofluoric acid in place of the wheel to remove unwanted areas of glass, and at the close of the decade limited use was being made of the process. One of their younger employees, John Northwood, was interested in this use of etching, hitherto normally employed in copper-plate-printing, and having an inventive mind considered he might improve on it. This he felt he could do more easily and profitably if he had his own business, and was therefore able to devote more time and attention to the problems involved.

By the early 1860s John Northwood had left his employer and was in partnership with his brother, Joseph, who attended to the office work. At premises they had erected at Wordsley, outside Stourbridge, they commenced a business concerned solely with decorating, executing ornament on wares sent to them by makers in the immediate area and farther afield.

They began with etching. This proved successful not only with the glass trade because of its comparative cheapness, but also with the public for the same reason and also because of its novel appearance. The process resulted in ornament differing from that previously available, the most noticeable feature being a delicacy of outline that could not be achieved by other methods. It relied on the use of workers with less skill than was required for engraving and cutting, and even if the acid was unpleasant and could be dangerous, labour costs were lower. Much of the finished work had a machine-like precision about it, but certain portions of patterns revealed by their flowing lines that they had, in essence, been drawn free-hand. An example is to be seen in Plate 34, in which the tendrils of the passion-flower could not have been rendered as realistically on the wheel. In contrast, the vine tendrils on the carafe in Plate 20, which were engraved, have a different and stiffer appearance. A feature of etched work is that the acid produces a curved, almost tubular, incision, so that an etched line looks as if it has raised edges. This is no more than an optical illusion, which can be checked by running a finger along such a line and finding that the surface is in reality perfectly flat.

John Northwood developed a lathe-like machine for the application of some of the more popular designs. With its use, borders of Greek Key, interlacing circles and similar running patterns were executed by men and women operatives after brief training. The article to be decorated was first coated inside and out with an acid-resistant waxy varnish, placed in the machine and a needle automatically cut the pattern through the protective layer. Placed in a bath of acid, the liquid was able to attack the glass surface only where it had been exposed by the needle, and after a period of immersion the varnish was removed and the work was complete.

More contrast could be given to the etched lines by using the engraver's wheel to provide areas of matt surface, and this was duly performed by the use of an acid mixture. Northwood also devised a method of etching the fashionable complex patterns of Greek and Renaissance inspiration. They were applied to articles by means of metal templates which guided the needle over the waxed surface, and once they had been cut out the templates could be stored for re-use whenever they might be required. When large-sized objects, such as ewers and dishes, were additionally embellished with matt areas by the use of what Northwood called his 'White Acid', the results were often impressive.

Equally active in executing decorative etching was the firm of Guest Brothers, of Brettell Lane, Stourbridge. One of the Guests had worked for a short time with Northwood before the latter decided to have his brother as sole partner. While the more important pieces from the Northwood workshop have been recorded and illustrated, those from

Guest's remain anonymous. No doubt the output of each decorating establishment had its characteristics, but time has blurred such subtleties and positive identification is very seldom possible.

It has been noted that classical vase shapes were frequently reproduced in glass in the 1850s. More than one firm relied on them for inspiration, but without always accompanying the form with the appropriate decoration; a version of the *oenochoë* was as likely to bear a pattern of irises as a band of nondescript ornament. Within a short time this interest in the ancient past extended to classical carvings in relief, and then to the imitations of them made in the second half of the eighteenth century by Josiah Wedgwood. Memory of him and his achievements had been revived in February 1845, when the Roman glass Portland vase was wantonly smashed while on display at the British Museum. As a result, the carefully-made Wedgwood copies of it, of which the first was made in 1790 and exhibited in a blaze of publicity, were recalled. The glass vase was repaired, the two hundred or so fragments being painstakingly re-assembled, and in September of the same year the Portland was again on view to the public.

A wider public interest was aroused in 1865 when the first volume of Eliza Meteyard's two-volume biography, *The Life of Josiah Wedgwood*, was published. In precisely the same year, the same title was used by Llewellyn Jewitt for a book covering the same ground, but written without the aid of important letters and other documents to which the author had been denied access. More tangible evidence of a revival of interest in the potter and his works was to be seen at the International Exhibition held in Paris in 1867, where the London firm of Wright & Mansfield gained an award for a large cabinet. The cabinet is of Adamesque neo-classical pattern, of satinwood mounted in gilt bronze and inset with eighteenth-century-style green and white Wedgwood plaques. It is now in the Victoria and Albert Museum.

The idea of reviving the production of relief ornament on glass, neglected since the days of the Romans, was a logical development. Its first nineteenth-century exponent was John Northwood, who was commissioned in 1864 to carve a vase made entirely of clear glass. The man who commissioned the work was J. B. Stone (later, Sir Benjamin Stone), partner in a Birmingham firm of glass-makers, Stone, Fawdry & Stone, who probably supplied Northwood with the basic vase. The finished object was presented to Birmingham City Art Gallery in 1876.

The vase, known as the Elgin vase, because it bears a central frieze in relief copied from the Elgin or Parthenon marbles, was not completed until 1873, nine years after its commencement. Above and below the frieze and on the handles, base and neck is etched ornament, and in the face of its imposing size (it stands 15½ in, 39·5 cm in height) it was hailed by a writer in a Worcestershire newspaper as 'probably the most important work produced since the famous Roman era'. Local pride may have induced an overstatement, but certainly the vase was the auspicious forerunner of an immense quantity of related glassware.

The Elgin vase was, as has been mentioned, entirely of clear glass, and its successful completion directed attention to the possibility of reviving true cameo glass in two colours. When the outer colour was cut away it revealed the contrasting colour of the inner body, and a really skilful craftsman could obtain delicate effects of light and shade comparable with those achieved by the long-dead and anonymous maker of the Portland vase.

There had apparently been talk in more than one glasshouse about the possibility of copying the Portland itself in its own medium. Not only would it be a feat in its own right, but if successful it could be relied on to gain enormous publicity for the maker and for the entire glass industry. There was no reason to doubt that it would be received far and wide with the same excitement as Wedgwood's copy had been nearly a century before.

It would seem that no one remembered an earlier and presumably successful attempt to make a modern copy of the vase only a few years previously. At the 1862 International Exhibition, held in London, such a vase had been displayed by Zach of Munich, but seemingly attracted no attention. On 3 December of the same year it appeared at Christie's, where it was sold by auction for £42. Thereafter, it vanished from record, and it may be wondered whether it is still in existence.

John Northwood's cousin, Philip Pargeter, had once been in partnership with Richardson, but in 1869 he gained the latter's business for himself. It has been reported that on an occasion when the cousins were talking, the conversation ran as follows: ' "John", said Philip to him one day, "I believe I can make the Portland Vase if you can decorate it". "I think I can", said Northwood, and so it was agreed between the two that the work should at once be put in hand'. One of Pargeter's employees named Daniel Hancocks or Hancox finally produced an acceptable blank, and it was then up to John Northwood to complete the task.

The making of a cameo blank began with the production of a small cup-shape in opaque white glass, of an amount sufficient for expansion into the finished article. While the cup was still hot, it was carefully filled with molten glass of the required contrasting colour; the latter being placed in the cup from the end of an iron on which it had been gathered from the pot. The bi-coloured mass was marvered to ensure fusion of the two glasses, re-heated at the mouth of the furnace and blown to the required size. It was then shaped and handles, if needed, were added. If all was successful, the annealed and cooled blank would be ready for the carver.

In earlier years, the making of cased articles had involved the application of only thin coatings, but for relief carving a thick outer coating was required and the operation was more complicated. The question of contraction while cooling was of particular importance, for if the properties of one of the glasses varied too greatly from those of the other the article would be likely to crack or scale. Additionally, the two layers had to fuse completely without any bubbles of air being trapped between them. Pinholes and similar small defects were to be avoided as far as possible, and the aim was always to make an absolutely flawless blank. In some instances, defects could not be detected until carving had reached an advanced stage, and if they could not be incorporated ingeniously into the design, then the project would have to be abandoned and a fresh start made.

The blank was first immersed in acid to give the surface a dull finish so that the design could be drawn on it. The parts that were to remain untouched were then protected with a coating of varnish, the interior was similarly treated all over and the article immersed in a bath of hydrofluoric acid. In due course, the unvarnished white portions were eaten away to reveal the coloured body, and the basic design remained silhouetted in relief.

Initially, the raised areas were shaped roughly on the wheel, but the bulk of the labour enjoyed neither mechanical nor chemical assistance. It has been described in some detail by John Northwood, jr, and was nothing if not tedious. He related how all the fine work was carved or sculptured as if the material was wood or stone. Pointed, hardened steel rods held in wooden handles were used, with reliance on hand-pressure and the assistance of carefully controlled taps from a light hammer or a mallet.

John Northwood had many difficulties with which to contend during the making of his copy of the Portland vase. Not least of them was the fact that the original was on public display in London, 120 miles distant, and while he would have had engravings for reference there is no record of any photographs being employed. It would seem not unlikely, however, that Northwood made use of them, for he was a photographer himself and would have realized how valuable such assistance could be.

At intervals during the three years in which the work progressed, Northwood took his vase to London for comparison with the prototype. There, the case containing the latter was opened for him, and he was able to see clearly what further details required attention. In 1876, when the end of the task was in sight, a further journey to London was about to be undertaken, and as the vase was being placed in its travelling-box it suddenly cracked. The action of momentarily holding the glass vessel in warm hands on a frosty morning was the cause, but the accident was not permitted to prevent completion of the work. Later, the crack extended so that the vase broke into two pieces, and it was then glued together. It was a most unfortunate ending after the expense of so much labour, but the result received high praise and the damage would seem to have been overlooked in the manner of the emperor's new clothes in Hans Andersen's story.

Following the completion of the task, Northwood executed another *tour de force*, the 'Pegasus' vase, known also as the 'Dennis' vase, for Thomas Wilkes Webb, proprietor of the Dennis glassworks at Stourbridge. The vase was constructed in three parts, stands 21 in (53·3 cm) in height and was given to the Smithsonian Institution, Washington, D.C., in 1929. The cover of the vase is surmounted by an equestrian figure of Pegasus, after one on a vase of which the frieze was designed by John Flaxman in 1784. A copy of the latter, described by Josiah Wedgwood as 'the finest and most perfect I have ever made', was presented by Wedgwood to the British Museum in 1786, and it is quite probable that Northwood saw it when he paid his earlier series of visits to the Museum.

The foregoing and other prestige pieces were exhibited and talked about, with the inevitable result that the public appetite was whetted for cameo glass. At the same time, demand for cut wares diminished, but the displaced craftsmen soon found employment in meeting the new requirement. Inevitably there was a shortage of really skilled men, those working for the Northwoods being tempted by offers of higher wages to go elsewhere in the neighbourhood. By about 1881, John Northwood was having to consider seriously whether he would not be well advised to close his workshop owing to the dearth of suitable staff. Just prior to that date, Frederick Carder, then no more than 17 or 18 years of age (he was born in 1863) began to show an interest in glass that duly resolved the situation.

Carder began his career by working in a pottery at Brierley Hill owned by his father and grandfather. He spent most of his evenings at local institutes studying art and other subjects, and at one of them made the acquaintance of John Northwood's son, also named John. As a result, Carder paid a visit to the Northwood decorating workshop where, among other things, he saw the Portland vase, of which he later wrote: 'When I saw this vase, I was struck by the possibilities of glass and determined, if possible, to get into the business.' On the recommendation of Northwood, sr, Carder was offered employment with Stevens and Williams, also of Brierley Hill, and in 1880 or 1881 left the pottery to work for the firm as a designer. Within a short time he was able to repay his indebtedness to John Northwood by mentioning that Northwood was thinking of closing his decorating shop. The latter was offered by Stevens and Williams the position of Works Manager and Art Director, which he accepted and held for the ensuing twenty years.

On account of his success in connection with the Council-owned Wordsley School of Art, Carder was sent in 1902 by South Staffordshire County Council to study glass-making in Germany and Austria. The visit was followed by another late in the following year, for the same purpose, which took him to the United States where, in March 1904, he was persuaded to settle at Corning, a town in New York State. A suitable building for his work was provided and he became founder of the Steuben Glass Works, later the Corning Glass Works, which gained international renown. To conclude, Carder retired in 1959, and died four years later at the age of 100.

At Brierley Hill, as well as elsewhere in the area, cameo glass soon became transformed from a one-off luxury decorating technique to one of mass production. The various processes were streamlined to ensure a cheaper and superficially attractive product. New body colours were devised, and at the same time the white outer layer was made thinner to save time and labour in removing unwanted areas. The Brierley Hill blanks were sent to Northwood's at Wordsley for decoration, while Webb's had their own workshop under the direction of the Woodall brothers, Thomas and George.

In attempts to speed-up production, makeshifts played a part, and health hazards received little attention. John Northwood, jr, described the acid-bath in these words: '... we made a stubby shaped handle out of wood and pitched it [stuck it with the aid of bitumen] to the bottom of the article. We had to keep removing the scum formed on the glass where acid was acting to prevent it eating down in an uneven way. To do this we had sticks of wood with a pad of cotton wool tied on the end which we called a "mop". The operation was to stand over the vat and whilst moving the article in the acid with the one hand, we rubbed the mop over the surface of the glass with the other. So you see we could not get very far away from the fumes. It was always an unpleasant job and no one wanted it.' He added that the vat stood in the open air or in an open shed in inclement weather, and that the fumes attacked the hands and faces of the unfortunate operators.

The two Woodall brothers had been employed by the Northwoods, and served their apprenticeship as engravers. They were, incidentally, nephews of Thomas Bott, who had begun his career as a painter of glass at Richardson's, and went in 1852 to carry out comparable work on china at the Worcester porcelain works. There, he became well known because of his porcelain painted in imitation of Limoges enamel, for which he received enthusiastic approval from the Prince Consort.

In about 1874 the Woodalls entered into employment at Webb's Dennis works. By then, the founder of the firm, Thomas Webb, had died, and his three sons were in charge. One of them had commissioned the Pegasus vases from Northwood, and by 1884 the Webbs were showing cameo glass of their own making. Among the pieces they displayed at the International Health Exhibition, held in London in that year, were some small plaques 'designed by George Woodall, formerly student at the Stourbridge School of Art, and manufactured by T. Webb and Sons, Stourbridge', which were purchased by the

Victoria and Albert Museum (Plate 38). For the remainder of the century, and later, the two Woodalls were responsible for producing numerous show-pieces for international exhibitions at which Webb's had stands, as well as works for sale to the general public.

Another craftsman who executed important cameo work was Alphone-Eugène Lecheverel, a Frenchman who was well known in his own country as a medallist and was brought to Stourbridge by Benjamin Richardson. Lecheverel came to England in about 1870 in order to teach cameo work to Richardson's employees, which he did over a period of about two years before returning to France. Only some half-dozen signed examples of his work have been recorded, two of them being among the specimens of glass at Brierley Hill Public Library.

Another man who gained a reputation for his cameo glass was Joseph Locke, who was born at Worcester and began work with the Stourbridge decorating firm of Guest Brothers in the late 1860s. Locke remained with Guest's for a few years and then went to Richardson's, but he also spent varying periods of time with other concerns in the Stourbridge area. For Richardson's he copied the Portland vase, the firm showing his example at the Paris International Exhibition in 1878. It has been recorded that between thirty and forty blanks were produced for the purpose, and that although carefully annealed, all but one of them fractured. The penultimate blank fell apart after Locke had started work on it, but he was fortunately able to achieve his aim with the one that remained. So much time had by then been expended that only six months were left before the exhibition opened, and although the vase was displayed before it was completely finished it gained a gold medal.

A variant of straightforward cameo decoration was patented by Webb's in 1887, the objective being to simulate old carved ivory. It was achieved by tinting the finished article 'with brown or other suitable colour, applying the colour more darkly in some parts than in others', and then fixing the colour in a kiln as if it was a piece of pottery. The vase illustrated in Plate 44 is an elaborated version of the 'Ivory Cameo' technique and is in the Persian style.

All the Stourbridge cameo glass is evidence of the skill and patience of its makers, and of the taste of the decades during which it was manufactured. Mythological subjects predominated for the prestige exhibition pieces, with semi-naked goddesses disporting themselves on vases, dishes and plaques. The majority of examples were signed by their executants and the more important were recorded in print at the time. In numerous instances the craftsmen achieved remarkable effects of light and shade, particularly where diaphanous scarves and similar covering were concerned, but the medium did not lend itself readily to the rendering of flowing lines. The human figure is too often depicted stiffly and with an expression that can only be described as wooden.

Natural subjects were usual on commercial articles, the representations ranging from garden and wild flowers to fruit, ferns and even seaweed. These were carved on large and small articles with grounds of many colours and when mounted in silver, as was the case, for instance, with scent bottles, they can be dated closely by means of the hallmarks. Exceptional pieces were made with more than one layer over the base colour, their making severely testing the skill of the blowers. Successful completion of these was a considerable feat and examples are scarce (Plate 39).

Cameo glass was not only made into articles for ornament since during the period in which it was produced there was a large market for articles for daily use. The more fashionable buyers continued to like Venetian-inspired wares, which they bought in versions made in Murano and imported or made in London by Powell's. The latter were superficially similar to the prototypes, but anglicized by having many of the 'frills' omitted.

In the late 1870s Macmillan's published a series of inexpensive books dealing with the home: the 'Art at Home' series, priced at 2s. 6d. (12½p) each, cloth-bound. One of them, entitled *The Dining Room* by Mrs Loftie, was intended, according to the Preface, 'for inexperienced housekeepers of small income, who do not wish to make limited means an excuse for disorder and ugliness'. She disapproved of much of the brightly-coloured glass in the shops at the time: 'Many of the specimens of glass in "rose pink" would scarcely give satisfaction anywhere to an eye which loved soft harmonies. The decoration is often flimsy or glaring. The opal is too strong and coarse in tone, and the pale blue too staring.' Equally, she found much of the coloured Venetian ware unpleasant, and blamed public demand for its popularity: 'the manufacturers, we feel sure, would prefer to meet a demand for articles in better taste'.

Mrs Loftie printed a full-page woodcut illustration of the types of

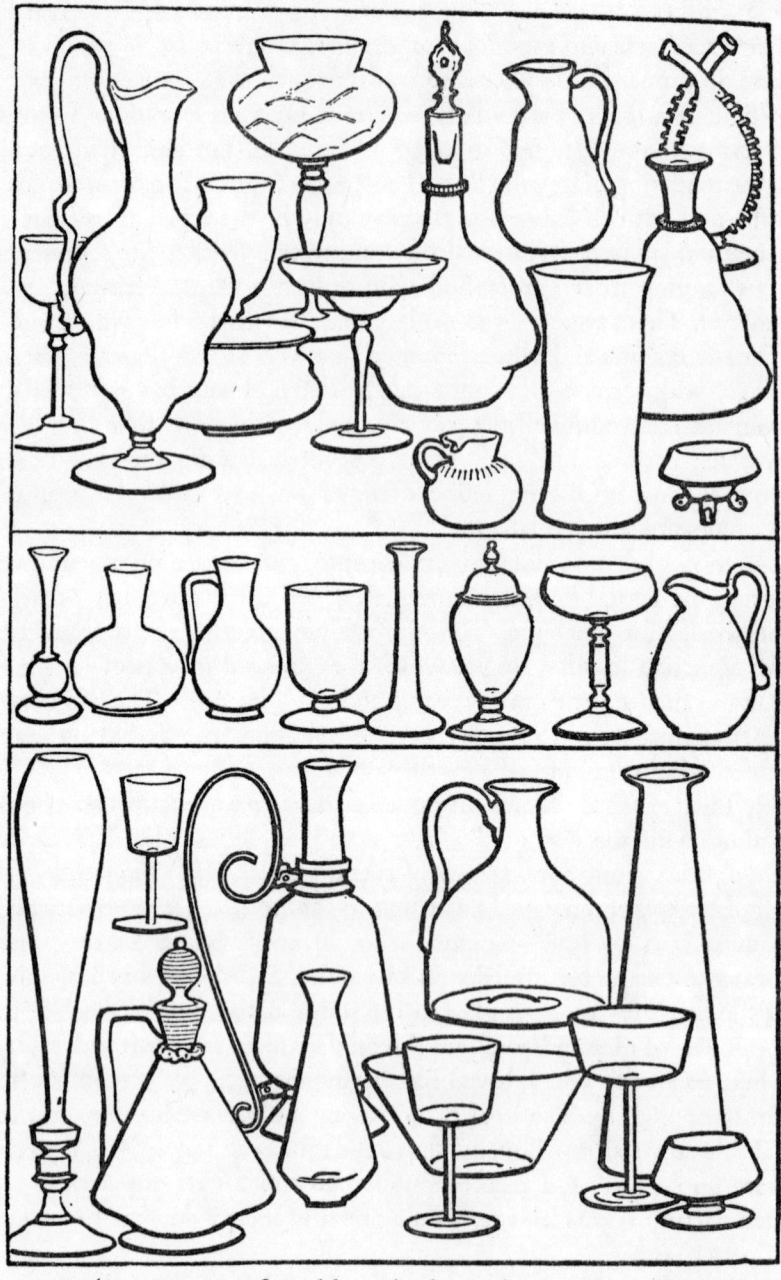

1. 'Specimens of Table Glass' made by Powell's of Whitefriars. From *The Dining Room* by Mrs Loftie, published in 1878.

glass then available and which she recommended, all of it from Powell's. Her comments on the articles ran as follows:

We have chosen the least expensive specimens. The price is very little in excess of that of the ugly and common glass to be had in every china shop. These patterns are not drawn to any particular scale, as space was valuable, and it was deemed unnecessary to give more than a mere outline showing the form distinctly. Most of these specimens are so accurately proportioned that they look equally well in any size. The same shape of jug, if it is good, will serve alike for tea, milk in the nursery, or water in the bedroom. . . . The importance of form cannot be too much insisted on. . . . The large cut needs little description, as it tells its own story. The only thing that may want an explanation is the double bottle at the right-hand corner. It is designed from an old English pattern, and was, we fancy, intended to hold cordials. . . . The water bottle like a hyacinth glass in the lowest division of the cut, has a little straight tumbler belonging to it that goes on the top . . . The decanter with the wide base is intended for use in a yacht.

Many of the shapes shown by Mrs Loftie would find admirers at any period, but the 'decanter for use in a yacht' may seem out of place in a book written for those living on small incomes. The wine glasses have all got the noticeably slender stems fashionable during the later 1870s. The authoress, who pays attention to every aspect of home life, refers to breakages during the washing-up of glass; a daily chore that accounts for the disappearance of so much. 'Breakage', she wrote, 'which might be lessened, particularly with wine-glasses, if the servant, in drying them, would hold the stem between his fingers, instead of placing the foot on the palm of the hand and screwing the top round till it comes off.'

The 'rose pink' glass referred to with such disapproval would have been the deep pinkish-red referred to today as ruby and in the United States as cranberry. Judging by the surviving quantity it must have been immensely popular for a long time. In addition to flower vases and ornamental objects, it was used for tumblers, wine glasses and jugs as well as salt cellars, sugar basins and other tableware. Many of the existing examples were probably imported, and quite a sizeable proportion of them probably reached England and elsewhere as late as the 1920s from factories on the mainland of Europe.

The red colour was obtainable in two ways: by adding to the batch either copper oxide or gold, the latter being dissolved in aqua regia – a mixture of nitric and hydrochloric acids. Inclusion of either of these did not immediately affect the clarity of the metal, it only acquired its colour when it was re-heated. In connection with the use of gold, a legend grew up that the red was produced by simply putting into the pot a gold sovereign straight from the pocket. For one or more of several reasons, to arouse comment, to induce good fortune or to display a sense of humour, it became customary in some glasshouses for the proprietor or manager to toss a coin into the pot. No doubt some of the more credulous onlookers believed that this affected the finished product, but modern investigation has shown that it did not. All that happened was that the coin melted and remained in the bottom of the pot without dispersing. D. R. Guttery wrote that 'Cribmen used to buy old pots from the glass-houses to recover for their own use such gold as was left in them'. Presumably this was any accumulated residue from the aqua regia mixture, in contrast to which the finding of the remains of a sovereign would have been a bonanza.

Some of the ruby or cranberry articles and those of other well-defined colours bear the so-called Mary Gregory decoration, in the form of painted representations of children more or less approximating to those popularized by Kate Greenaway. The work was only seldom done with much care, and in most instances was executed entirely in opaque white, sometimes with flesh-colour for faces and hands and occasionally with borders of bright gilding. The true Mary Gregory was a decorator employed by the Boston & Sandwich Glass Company, of Sandwich, Massachusetts, in the 1870s. She favoured silhouettes in white of the type mentioned, but an immense amount of ware in her manner originated in Central Europe. Not all of it was made in the nineteenth century, as examples have been noted inscribed beneath the base with the legend 'Made in Czechoslovakia'; a country that did not come into existence until October 1918.

As an alternative, the ruby glass was ornamented with clear glass to provide contrasting rims, bases, feet and handles. The coloured body was first formed, and then the additions were affixed and tooled by hand. John Northwood, jr, wrote of a Stourbridge liking in the 1880s

50. Vase and jug of milk-white glass with applied coloured fruit and flower ornament. Late-nineteenth century. Heights: 10 and 16·5 cm. *Mrs. A. Buckingham.*

51. Flower holder in opalescent topaz-coloured glass. Late-nineteenth century. Height: 14·2 cm. *Mrs. A. Buckingham.*

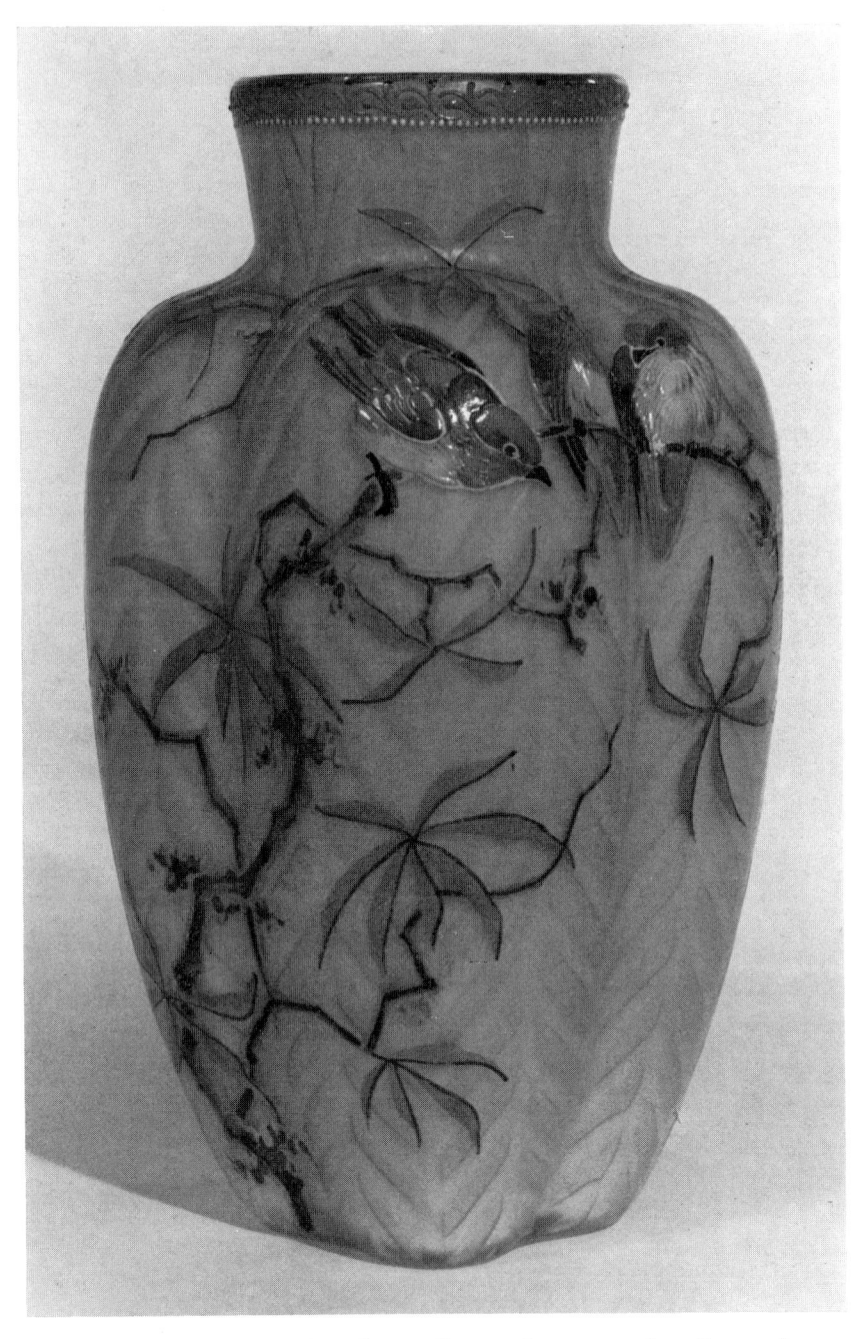

52. Vase, shading in colour from yellow at the top to pale yellow at the base, the rim blue and the whole with a satin finish, enamelled and gilt with birds on a branch of bamboo. About 1880. Height: 21·3 cm. *Sotheby's Belgravia.*

53. Jug of opaque white over clear glass overlaid with pale blue to form a diamond-shaped air-trap pattern, and the whole with a satin surface. About 1880. Height: 24 cm.

54. Vase of Queen's Burmese ware shading from pink at the neck to yellow at the base, marked QUEEN'S BURMESE WARE PATENTED, about 1890. Height: 20·6 cm. *Sotheby's Belgravia.*

55. Table centrepiece with flower holders and two 'Fairy' nightlights in Queen's Burmese ware painted with flowers and berries, marked THOs. WEBB & SONS QUEEN'S BURMESE WARE PATENTED and S. CLARKE'S FAIRY PATENT TRADEMARK, about 1890. Height: 24·8 cm. *Sotheby's Belgravia.*

56. Chandelier for eight lights in clear glass decorated with ruby and green, by James Powell & Sons, London, 1865. *Victoria and Albert Museum.*

57. Decanter in green-tinted glass designed by T. G. Jackson in 1870 and made by Powell's. Height: 26·5 cm. *Victoria and Albert Museum.*

58. Flower vase, the fan-shaped bowl in opalescent topaz-coloured glass and the stem in amber, probably made by Powell's in about 1880. Height: 27·8 cm. *Mrs. P. Julyan.*

59. Glass made in the Venetian style by James Powell & Sons, London, in 1876. Height: 17·5 cm. *Victoria and Albert Museum.*

60. Glass perhaps for champagne, made in the Venetian style by Powell's in 1876. Height: 16.2 cm. *Victoria and Albert Museum.*

61. Vase of clear glass partially layered in red, brown and yellow and engraved in Rock Crystal style with a pattern of plums and foliage, by William Fritsche, about 1885. Height: 14·7 cm. *Kunstmuseum, Düsseldorf.*

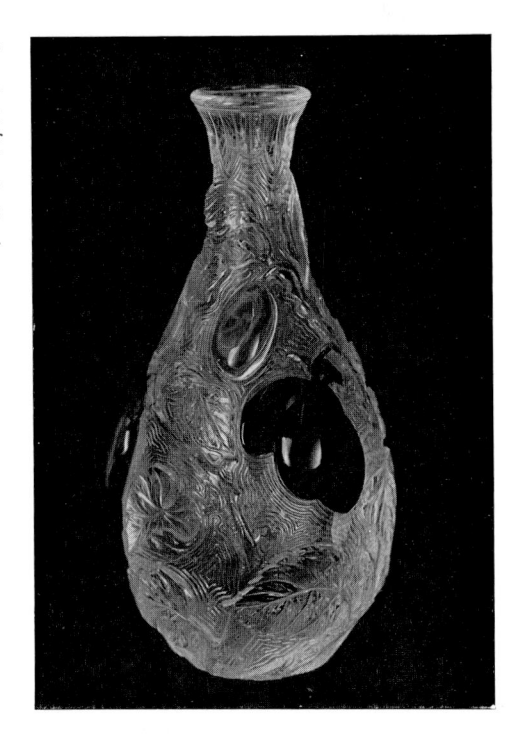

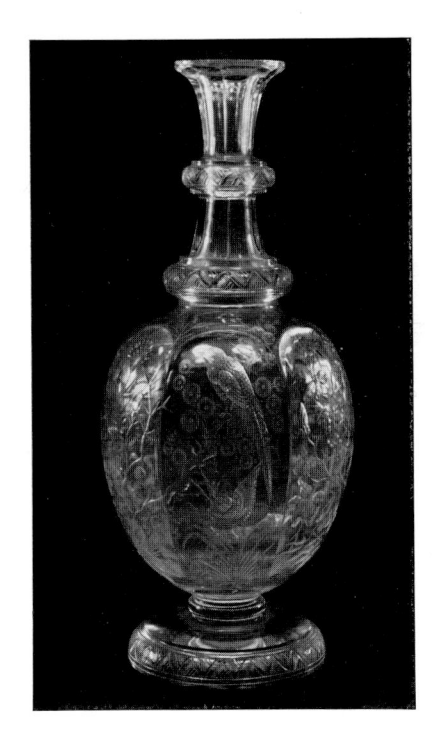

62. Vase engraved in Rock Crystal style with panels of birds and plants, probably made by Stevens & Williams of Brierley Hill and engraved by Joseph Keller, about 1885. Height: 26·7 cm. *Sotheby's Belgravia.*

63. Two specimen flower holders in clear glass: (left) with engraved decoration, and (right) with the surface rendered matt in an acid-bath. Heights: 12·7 and 14·9 cm.

64. Dish in colourless glass press-moulded with the heads of Victoria and Albert. Mid-nineteenth century. Diameter: 10 cm. *Alan Buckingham, Esq.*

65. Dish for grapes, press-moulded in opaque white glass with a satin finish, marked PATENTED AUG 31 1875. Length: 19·7 cm.

66. Flower vase of transparent blue glass in the form of two upraised hands holding flowers and foliage, about 1880. Height: 13 cm.

67. Three pieces of press-moulded cream-coloured ware made by Sowerby's of Gateshead: (left) vase lettered round the rim 'Mary, Mary quite contrary'; (centre) trough patterned with Kate Greenaway-style children depicting 'Mary had a little lamb'; and (right) vase with panels of parrots on branches. About 1880. Heights: 14, 15·8 and 15·2 cm. *Laing Art Gallery and Museum, Newcastle upon Tyne.*

68. Vase, press-moulded in brown and white marbled glass by Sowerby's, Gateshead, about 1880. Height: 7 cm. *Laing Art Gallery and Museum, Newcastle upon Tyne.*

69. Vase, press-moulded in peacock-blue and green variegated glass, pattern No. 1244 in Sowerby's 1882 Pattern Book (see page 62). Height: 10.8 cm. *Laing Art Gallery and Museum, Newcastle upon Tyne.*

70. Receptacle in the form of a basket, press-moulded in opaque pale blue glass by Sowerby's of Gateshead, about 1880. Length: 12·7 cm.

71. Sugar basin in opalescent yellow ('vaseline') glass made by Davidson's of Gateshead, the design registered in 1891. Height: 10·4 cm. *Laing Art Gallery and Museum, Newcastle upon Tyne.*

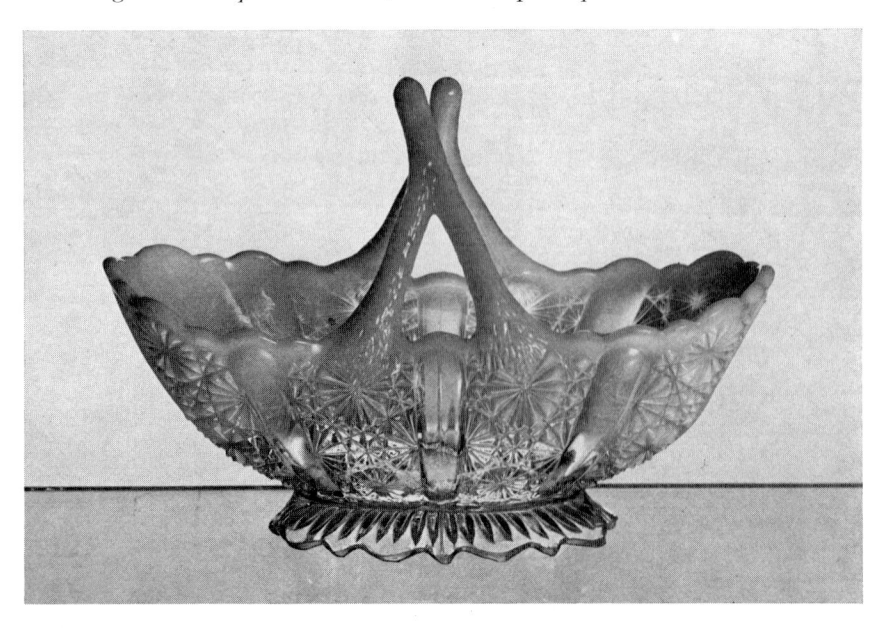

72. Dish in colourless glass press-moulded with a design commemorating the Jubilee of Queen Victoria's accession, 1887, the design registered at the Patent Office by Sowerby's of Gateshead. Diameter: 25·1 cm. *Victoria and Albert Museum.*

73. Two boats of press-moulded glass: (top) pen-tray and stand in amber-colour, and (bottom) receptacle in clear glass. Lengths: 26·3 and 12·7 cm.

74. Vase with vertically-ribbed body and handles surmounted by pincered discs, the neck with a collar pincered at intervals, made by Sowerby's, Gateshead, about 1880. Height: 17·5 cm. *Laing Art Gallery and Museum, Newcastle upon Tyne.*

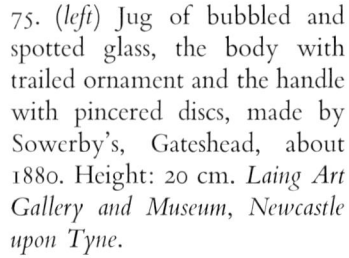

75. (*left*) Jug of bubbled and spotted glass, the body with trailed ornament and the handle with pincered discs, made by Sowerby's, Gateshead, about 1880. Height: 20 cm. *Laing Art Gallery and Museum, Newcastle upon Tyne.*

76. (*Below*) Vase made of glass with opalescent streaks, bubbles and chemical inclusions, designed by Christopher Dresser for James Couper & Sons, Glasgow, about 1870. Marked CLUTHA DESIGNED BY D C REGISTERED. Height: 8 cm. *Sotheby's Belgravia.*

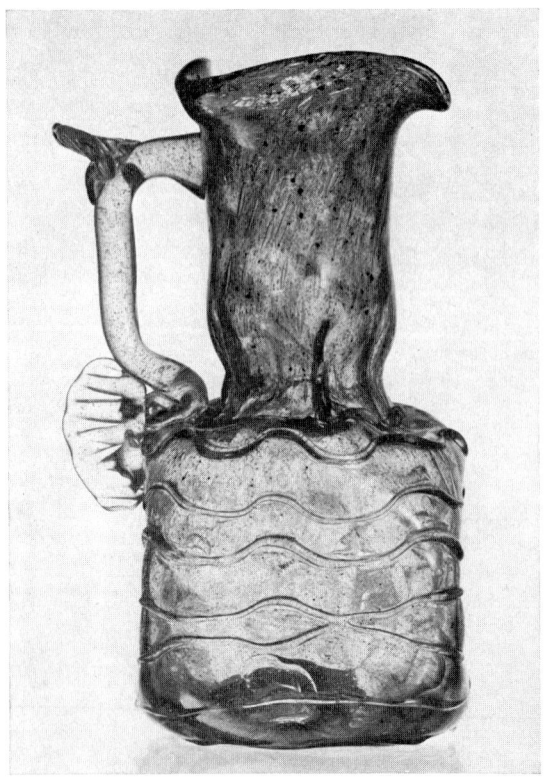

77. Set of six tumblers and a jug in clear glass with silver mounts, the latter hallmarked 1882, designed by Christopher Dresser. Height of jug: 22·2 cm. *Victoria and Albert Museum.*

78. Two rolling-pins: (top) splashed with red and blue on opaque white, and (bottom) dark green splashed with white. Lengths: 30·5 and 39·3 cm. *County Museum, Truro, Cornwall.*

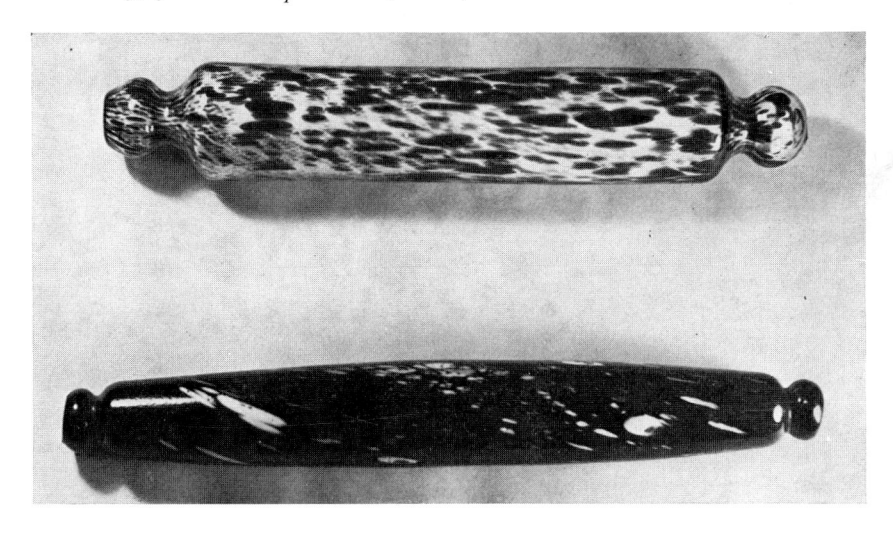

79. Flask of striped red, white and blue glass with a pewter mount and screw cap. Length: 20·3 cm. *County Museum, Truro, Cornwall.*

80. Five coloured glass hand-bells. Average height: 28 cm. *Sotheby's.*

for making small vases of tinted glass with applied leaves, the latter having frilled edges rather like those of an acanthus. His description of how they were made shows how much the appearance of the finished articles relied on the handiwork and judgment of their makers.

The body of the article – a vase, a bowl, etc. – was shaped with a rounded base and usually had a crimped or scalloped top. To form the leaf a youth brought the glassmaker a piece of hot glass on the end of his gathering iron, the glass being cylindrical in shape. The glassmaker stuck the end of this on the underside of the article, and stretching and pulling this out he left a small length of it hanging loose, then, still drawing it thinner, stuck it to the body or side of the vase in a sloping direction and trailing it off to a point. Thus was formed the main stem, or centre, of the leaf, and the small loose loop formed one of the feet of the vase. There would be three of these leaves made round the body and so they would make the three feet which the vase would stand on.

When the main stem was stuck on the vase, the youth would bring another piece of hot glass, which the maker would proceed to stick up alongside this stem, repeating the process on the other side of the stem, then whilst it was still pliable, with suitable tools, he pressed these sides into leaf forms and so was made one large-sized leaf.

Northwood stated that the design was very popular, 'for many thousands were made of all shapes and sizes'. He added that some were sold in their bright state, as they left the hands of the maker, but many were dipped in acid to give them a matt surface. Examples, which are now no longer so plentiful, are easily recognized by their three curled feet from which spring large nearly-pointed leaves attached to the sides of the vase.

5
Press-moulded and other late varieties

The Stourbridge makers continued to devise novelties in colour and form, introducing fresh techniques as well as reviving and adapting old ones. In the mid-1880s Japanese influence, which was to be seen in the home in the shape of fans and asymmetrical furniture led to glass vases with applied ornament resembling gnarled tree branches. Stevens & Williams marketed their version under the name of *Matsu no Ke*, which can be translated as 'The Spirit of the Pine Tree' in acknowledgment of the sylvan inspiration. The name is perhaps the most oriental feature of the articles that were made by more than the one firm, many examples sharing a fragility that has ensured a high proportion of damaged survivors.

Among the more realistic of variations on the preceding type are those hung with cherries and other fruit, the glistening glass effectively simulating the real thing (Plate 50). A large proportion of the output of the time, the foregoing excepted, was matt-surfaced, so that the true quality of the glass was not apparent. In fact, during much of the Victorian period it was fashionable for the material to resemble anything other than itself. The majority of the pale-coloured and matt-textured specimens have a close resemblance to tinted icing sugar, but they undoubtedly satisfied the taste of the public at the date they were made and there is no lack of enthusiastic collectors nowadays.

Other fancy articles embodied *latticinio* work, a technique that had been exploited earlier in England in the stems of wine glasses, and now used more widely as in Venice. The effect was achieved with the aid of a mould having a ridged interior against which were stood rods of opaque white or coloured glass, as required. The craftsman then blew a sphere of clear glass into the mould, picking up the rods and withdrawing them from the mould adhering to the bubble. The latter was marvered to embed the rods, and then blown to shape and manipulated in the normal manner. In the course of the work, the rods became stretched until they were mere threads, the finished article having a pattern of lacy lines within a clear body.

A further introduction involved making an article with a patterned body by blowing molten glass into a suitable mould. The pattern was usually of simple straight lines or a trellis, and this was entirely covered with an outer layer of tinted transparent glass. The air trapped in the furrows between the layers formed a subtle design, and the effect was accentuated by giving the exterior a matt surface. This style of decoration was popular from about 1880 onwards, the product being sometimes referred to nowadays as quilted glass. Alternatively, because of the matt finish it is termed *verre de soie* or 'satin glass', but that name is equally applicable to other wares that lack the air-trapped ornament.

Covering a surface with closely-wound threads of glass, often in a colour different from that of the body of the article, was another type of decoration. It was used mostly between 1860 and 1880, when there was also a vogue for ribbed feet and handles on jugs and much else. Such fashions, like so many others, were very seldom confined to any single maker, and even if a design was patented it took one or more competitors only a short time to produce a close copy that did not infringe the rights of the original.

Experiments continued to be carried out in many countries, each imitating the success of another and occasionally manufacturing under legal licence from a patentee. An example of this last occurred with the so-called 'Burmese' glass, which was devised by Frederick S. Shirley, of the Mount Washington Glass Company, New Bedford, Massachusetts. The glass was opaque, and shaded in each specimen from a pale yellow to a rich pink and was left with a natural shine or given a matt finish. Patented in December 1885, Burmese relied for its colouring on the inclusion among its ingredients of uranium oxide and gold. When fused, the batch produced a yellow-tinted glass, but re-heating turned it red and partial re-heating resulted in the bi-coloured Burmese.

The American firm patented their ware in England in June 1886, and a licence to manufacture it was obtained by Webb's. At about the same date the Mount Washington concern presented Queen Victoria with some pieces of the glass. In return, the Queen ordered a tea-service of forty-five pieces together with four vases and a bowl, the tea-set being described at the time as being ornamented with flowers or vines in colours and gold.

Webb's purchase proved a judicious one, and they wisely took full advantage of the Royal interest in it by naming their product 'Queen's Burmese Ware'. Some was sold plain allowing the colouring to provide its own decoration, but much of it was painted and gilded. Many pieces bear a circular etched mark beneath the base with the wording 'THO^s WEBB & SONS BURMESEWARE PATENTED R^d 80167'; others have a similar legend impressed, or printed on a paper label. Vases and other ornaments were made by Webb's, who used Royal Burmese also for making shades for Samuel Clarke's patented 'Fairy' nightlights. These became highly fashionable for lighting the dinner table and were sometimes combined with flower-holders to form a central feature (Plate 55).

Each 'Fairy' shade was supplied with a clear glass base on which to stand one of Clarke's candles, and they could be bought in any quantity as single items without floral attachments. Plain, striped, shaped and inset with 'jewels', the shades were made in many forms and colours in England and elsewhere. They enjoyed a short-lived popularity that was eclipsed by the more versatile and safer electricity; their introduction dated from 1886 and by about 1892 their vogue was at an end.

Another type of table centrepiece was a modernized version of the eighteenth-century silver epergne, but this time made of glass. In most instances the Victorian version comprised a tall and slender vase surrounded by a series of shaped arms from which were suspended small baskets. Examples in clear glass appeared during the 1860s, but by the beginning of the next decade colour was being added and the baskets were suspended from arms in the shape of leaves. In most instances the various portions, vases and leaves, were assembled on a base made with holes into which each fitted, the base sometimes in the form of a rosebowl. In others, the base was a flat mirror with a bevelled edge, known at the time as a 'plateau'.

Not all such articles were products of the bigger glasshouses, and as was the case with many of the other wares quite a few came from the enterprising craftsmen who ran cribs. Of one of them, named Tom Jukes, it has been recorded by D. A. Guttery that he made 'wonderfully coloured and fashioned ware, particularly those many-branched flower-stands with their trumpet vases (the gaffers called them "carrots") which were best-sellers'.

The pointed leaves featured on so many of the stands were imitated from earlier Venetian pieces, on which they were often made in a clear glass rimmed with pink, blue or green. As early as 1864 or 1865 Powell's of Whitefriars had made a chandelier closely copying this Venetian style, with incised-twist arms, moulded nozzles and grease-pans, and ornamental leaves at the top and round the centre of the stem (Plate 56). It was some ten years before leaves of the same kind began to appear from the Stourbridge glasshouses, many of which served a less sophisticated market than was supplied from the capital.

Powell's not only followed the Venetians in many of their wares, but also made a number of pieces especially designed in England. The decanter in Plate 57 was the work of an architect, T. G. Jackson (later, Sir Thomas Graham Jackson, R.A.), who did much work on buildings at Oxford and Cambridge. The decanter is part of a set of table-ware designed by him in 1874, the year in which, incidentally, he was engaged in restoring a church at Annesley, Nottinghamshire. Whereas Philip Webb's earlier glasses for William Morris have been described as having 'a somewhat Gothic cast of design', Jackson's show no hint of the favoured ecclesiastical building style. The decanter appears in the upper part of the woodcut, Fig. 1 on page 50, and other vessels shown near the decanter would seem to have come from the same source. Certainly, many of them follow the same general lines, for example, the carafe on the right.

Under the direction of Harry J. Powell, who was in charge of the Whitefriars glassworks from 1880, a considerable quantity of meritorious pieces in plain and tinted metal was produced. Venice continued to be the dominant influence to the very end of the century, when there was a liking for impracticably tall, slender-stemmed wine glasses. They were more fitted for display in cabinets than for use at table, but their design was often highly imaginative, the colours good and the workmanship excellent.

A further Venetian speciality was also successfully imitated by Powell's during the last decade of the century. In 1857–58, G. G. Scott (later, Sir George Gilbert Scott, R.A.) built the Chapel at Exeter College, Oxford, including in the interior decoration some glass mosaics by Antonio Salviati. The same architect was also responsible for some of Salviati's mosaic work being used in the reredos in Westminster Abbey, London. The coloured cubes of glass for the work were imported from Venice, the success of the undertaking doing much to enhance the reputations of both Murano and Salviati.

Later, Salviati executed some mosaics in St Paul's Cathedral. They were made to the designs of G. F. Watts, R.A. and were placed in the spandrels of the dome, where they provided a touch of colour in what Queen Victoria described in 1872 as a building that was 'dull, cold, dreary and dingy'. In 1890 a further suggestion was made with regard to St Paul's, this time it was to decorate the arches of the choir, the sanctuary and the choir proper. The artist selected to prepare designs was W. B. Richmond (later, Sir William Bruce Richmond, R.A.).

He was led to select glass mosaic for the purpose because of the atmosphere in the city at that date, stating that 'while London maintains its reputation as the dirtiest capital in the world, while authorities continue to allow the air to be polluted with smoke, decorations must undergo an annual spring cleaning'. Glass was, therefore, preferable to other mediums, and Richmond set to work with a will. He was a man of firmly-rooted ideas, and two of his specific demands were that only British workers should be employed on the project and none of them should belong to a trade union. In connection with his insistence on the latter condition, it was reported that at one stage of the proceedings 'he observed an unaccountable slacking off in their enthusiasm, the cause of which, however, was not far to seek. A member of a Trade Union had been engaged unawares; the black sheep was dismissed, and the work progressed satisfactorily as before.' Richmond insisted not only on the employment of British hands, but on the use of British materials. To this end, he consulted Harry J. Powell, who made numerous experiments to produce exactly what was required. Coloured opaque glass was finally cast into slabs measuring about 6 in square by a $\frac{1}{2}$ in thick (15·2 cm square by 13 mm), which were then broken into small cubes by using a pair of metal sugar-nippers: at that time in current use, but nowadays looked upon as an interesting 'antique'. Gold and silver cubes were made from slabs with thin leaves of the metals laid on them, and covered with a protective coating of clear glass. The area to be covered was no less than 26,000 ft^2 (2,175 m^2), and the total number of cubes used to cover it ran into millions.

When the work was eventually completed, the critics and the public in general, were not pleased with the result of Richmond's lengthy labours. *The Times* wrote of a storm raging about him concerning what was termed the 'decorative destruction' of the Cathedral, and like other artists in comparable situations he was bitterly disappointed by the lack of appreciation accorded his achievement. He was angry, too, at the lack of proper illumination within the building, so that the mosaics could be viewed only occasionally in such dim natural light as penetrated to where they were placed. Richmond wrote in his typical style about this: 'Even upon a bright summer day the interior of St. Paul's is veiled by a smoke which is never absent. This has to be taken into account till the authorities prohibit it. Smoke has been a nuisance to London for three hundred years, but no Government has been strong enough to make it a penal offence.' Fifty or so years after he had penned those words, long after his death in 1921, Richmond's taunt at governmental weakness was at last inapplicable, and the causing of smoke in London was made a punishable offence.

Despite all the trouble taken to ornament the Cathedral and the publicity it must have afforded English-made glass and English craftsmanship, the use of mosaic did not become widespread. Although Richmond played his part with sincerity, his pugnacious attitude may well have contributed in some degree to its failure.

Although there were many innovations following the repeal of the excise duty in 1845, the traditional taste for clear cut glass did not entirely die throughout Victoria's reign. Even when the demand for carved cameo work was at its strongest, there remained a lively market for the products of talented cutters and occasionally fresh surges of interest in that type of ornament.

German and Bohemian glass-engravers and cutters had been coming to England from about 1850 onwards, and one in particular who arrived during the decade following achieved considerable success. He was a Bohemian, Frederick Kny, who worked for Webb's of Stourbridge, on whose premises he had his own workshop and presumably thereby retained a degree of independence. In about 1880 he was among the first to execute decoration in a new manner, named 'Rock Crystal' engraving, which gained its name from a likeness to work on the natural stone.

It was, perhaps, not unpredictable that the designers and craftsmen of the day should turn to crystal for inspiration after they had so wholeheartedly demonstrated their admiration for its imitator, Venetian glass. This, in turn, by its very name *cristallo*, had been inspired by rock crystal, and the principal endeavour of its makers had been to simulate the latter as closely as possible. The Venetians, however, had only their soda glass, which did not lend itself easily to copying the brilliant clarity of the original. The German metal, with potash as its alkaline constituent, was much closer to nature, and the traditional skills of the lapidaries of the country were used in the same manner with great success. That had been in the early sixteenth century, and such work continued to be executed for the next hundred years or so.

Until Kny and his fellow immigrants attempted the task, no one had tried to use English lead glass in the same way. The result was certainly successful, but limited in appeal because of its cost and perhaps also because the public still preferred the hobnail and other geometrical cuts with which it had been familiar for so long.

The outstanding requirement of Rock Crystal engraving was the weight of glass needed in any vessel that was to receive it. The finished piece gave the impression of having been cut from a solid lump, leaving the walls thick and with the ornamentation highly polished. The actual engraving, or cutting, was not always deep, and in many instances did not extend more than a millimetre or so below the surface. Designs ranged from imitations of Renaissance vessels, complete with fierce-looking bearded male masks concealing pouring-lips, to pseudo-Japanese compositions of birds and flowers (Plate 62).

Frederick Kny soon had a fellow immigrant, William Fritsche, nearby in another workshop at Webb's. At Stevens & Williams, were Joseph Keller and Frank Scheibner, and doubtless there were other men at Stourbridge working in the same manner whose names are no longer remembered. A proportion of surviving examples are signed and this has enabled attributions of anonymous ones to be made. In other cases the particular style of a craftsman is known and can occasionally be recognized.

It has been noted earlier that some machine-pressed glassware was being manufactured in Stourbridge in the 1850s, and a certain amount continued to be produced in later years. It was, however, for high quality hand-made goods that the town became known, and its reputation for them continues to this day, with descendants of many of the Victorian makers still active in the area.

Elsewhere in England, press-moulded articles were in production from as early as the 1830s, with output being concentrated on such things as plates and tumblers. For these there was not only a ready sale, but they were especially suitable for the method of manufacture. Birmingham, Warrington and Manchester were among the towns boasting factories that turned out goods of the type; all of them situated where there were large populations to provide a quick sale and with a minimum of transport costs to be faced. Utilitarian articles continued to be made at those places, the majority of the output designed with simulated cutting of the kind seen on expensive ware, but it was in the north-east of England that fresh developments duly took place.

The area had been a glass-making centre from at least the early seventeenth century, when craftsmen from Lorraine are known to have been established there. At that date, the use of timber as a fuel for furnaces was being officially discouraged, but with ample coal immediately to hand this was no hindrance. By the year 1700, Newcastle had acquired a reputation for its Crown window glass, although a writer of the time described it as 'subject to have Specks and Blemishes and Streaks in it, and 'tis very often warped crooked'. The discs, known as 'tables' were packed in light wooden cases, each containing between thirty-five and forty-five, which were sent to London in the coasters taking coal to the capital: 'they being set on end in the Coles more than half its depth, by which means they are kept steady from falling and being broke by the motion, and rowling of the Ship'.

By the mid-eighteenth century wine glasses were being made at Newcastle, and besides distribution in England were exported to the Netherlands and Scandinavia. A century later, in the 1850s, the district had returned mainly to making sheet glass, not only by the Crown process, but also employing the Broad process and casting. At a later date, some decorative and useful wares in the Venetian style were made, but it was the exploitation of press-moulding that led to the production of immense quantities of articles that were acceptable to the public and profitable to the makers.

Clear flint glass was the medium that was first employed, but much of the early output was marred by flaws; rough edges where the molten metal had been squeezed through gaps in hinged moulds, and defects caused by the metal cooling too rapidly for the press to be fully effective. These and other faults were gradually overcome, some of them being minimized by the introduction of complex patterns with dotted grounds against which they were at least less obvious. By the time the north-country makers turned their attention to the process its development was well advanced.

The firms in the north-east sprang into prominence in the course of the 1870s, when the three leading makers found that there was a public liking for a particular variety of opaque, marbled glass that had, in fact, been on the market more or less unnoticed for about a quarter of a century. The material, known as Slag glass because one of its constituents was the waste slag from iron works, resembled anything but glass, but the firms concerned also made goods in a range of plain colours as well as in clear glass.

The largest of the factories was at Gateshead, known as Sowerby & Neville from about 1855 to 1872, as Sowerby & Co. from about 1872 to 1881, and as Sowerby's Ellison Glass Works from December 1881 onwards. In 1882, they were described as owning the biggest pressed-glass works in the world, with between 700 and 1,000 employees. Each worked a seven-hour shift, and it was stated that a man could produce 1,100–1,200 tumblers per shift.

The firm's pattern book of the same year announced that they manufactured a varied assortment of goods: 'Opal, Turquoise, Gold, Jet, Venetian in several colours. Giallo, Blanc-de-lait, Malachite – Patent

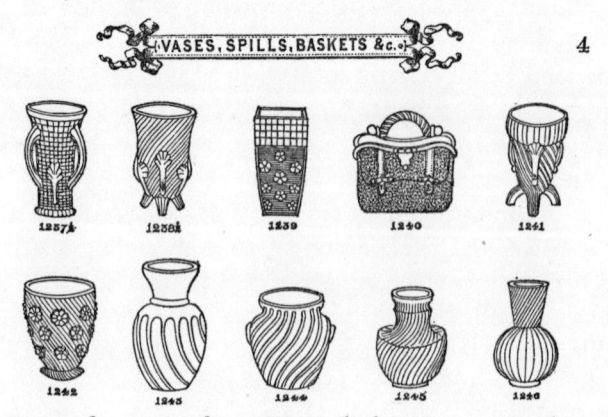

2. Part of a page from Sowerby's Pattern Book, 1882. The centre vase in the lower row (no. 1244) is illustrated in Plate 69.

Ivory Queen's Ware – Decorated·Opaque·Stained·Blanc-de-lait, and new Tortoise Shell Ware.' It added that they had offices at Gateshead, London, Birmingham, Paris and Hamburg. An earlier catalogue described all except the jet goods under the heading 'Vitro-Porcelain', which literally translates as 'glass-porcelain'. This is perhaps a fair term for a material that is glass but does not resemble it, and that might appear to a casual observer to be a kind of chinaware.

Sowerby's marked a proportion of their products from about 1876 onwards, using a crest in the form of a peacock's head, in relief. When it occurs it is usually located beneath the base of an article, but occasionally it is in the interior. They also registered many of their designs with the Patent Office, using the diamond-shaped mark that verifies the fact. The mark, with the letters and numerals in the corners to indicate the date of registration and other details, gives the actual date on which the pattern was given legal protection. It does not imply that a piece was made in that very month and year, as patterns remained in use over a varied period of time that might extend to a decade or more. Many books of marks on pottery and porcelain give information about deciphering the patent marks, but the latter are not always easy to read.

A few miles from Gateshead was the Wear Glass Works, Sunderland, owned by Henry Greener & Co. They made similar goods to

3. Marks on pressed wares made by *(top left)* Sowerby's, *(top right)* Greener's and *(bottom)* Davidson's. The marks are in relief and each measures about 6mm long.

Sowerby's, advertising in 1881 that their range of colours included 'blue, green, amber, puce, blue and black, Majolica and Malachite'. It is hard to imagine what 'Majolica' can have looked like, as it normally describes a type of polychrome-decorated pottery and not any single colour. By 1884, Greener's were also using a crest mark in relief, in this instance a demi-lion holding a battleaxe.

The third of the firms was George Davidson & Co. of Teams Glass Works, Gateshead, which made similar wares to the other two. In addition, Davidson's made their 'Pearline', which was partly opalescent in contrast to the body colour. This was often a shade of blue, but other colours have been recorded, including a yellow. The name, but not the material, was exclusive to Davidson's, as other firms made a very similar product. The mark used was, once again, a crest in relief: a demi-lion issuing from a mural coronet. Much of the output was unmarked except for the Patent Office registration mark, which enables examples bearing it to be traced to their maker. It may be mentioned that Davidson's have, within recent years, re-started production of some pressed wares and these can prove deceptive to the unwary. Marked pieces examined have a much glossier finish than old ones, but the passage of time can well make the new indistinguishable from the old.

The designs found in pressed glass, whether from the north-east of England or elsewhere in the country, reflect the times in which they were current. Imitations of basket-weaves vied with ribbing as a background to panels modelled in low relief with figures in the manner of Kate Greenaway, whose activity as an artist commenced in about 1870 and lasted until her death in 1901. Inevitably, there were also willowy Japanese ladies, and oriental plants. The easiest to date accurately are the numerous commemorative dishes and other articles made on the occasions of Queen Victoria's Jubilee, the death of W. E. Gladstone, and whenever an event offered a ready sale. Most of these items were in transparent glass, usually tinted but sometimes clear, with a pattern of dots on the underside to produce an attractively glittering message. Early and late examples are illustrated in Plates 64 and 71, the one commemorating Queen Victoria's wedding in 1840 and the other her Jubilee in 1887.

Sowerby's also attempted to find a niche in the market for handmade glass. A number of examples showing the ubiquitous Venetian influence have survived, among the more ambitious being the two-handled vase in Plate 74. The body is ribbed, has an applied pincered neck-band, and the handles are topped by discs. It is a long way from Venice and from Powell's, but the inspiration is there even if it has become somewhat diluted.

Of approximately the same date is the jug in Plate 75. It again embodies some of the techniques just mentioned; the tooled disc below the handle and the thumb-piece at the top, while the whole is encircled with bands of trailed ornament. However, no longer is the body of the piece of simple outline, it is better described as eccentric, and the metal of which it is formed is streaked and bubbled. Not many years earlier such a piece would have been cast aside as worthless, but suddenly the pendulum of fashion was swinging from the balanced to the unbalanced, and from flawless metal to a deliberate cultivation of blemishes.

Sowerby's and some of the other glass-makers of the time were perhaps recalling John Ruskin's words written some thirty years earlier. He had then stated: '. . . no delicate outlines are to be attempted, but only such fantastic and fickle grace as the mind of the workman can conceive and execute on the instant. The more wild, extravagant, and grotesque in their gracefulness the forms are, the better.' It is very doubtful if the pronouncement was taken literally. These rough-looking and apparently accidental articles would not have been left just to the whim of a craftsman, but were as much a product of the drawing-board as any other goods.

The best known of pieces in the style were made from about 1885 by the Glasgow firm of James Couper & Sons, who gave theirs the trade name 'Clutha': Gaelic for cloudy. Much of their output was designed by Christopher Dresser, in which case each article bore beneath the base an etched legend: 'Clutha designed by C.D. registered'.

Dresser, who was born in Glasgow in 1834, began his career as a lecturer in botany. By 1862, he had changed course and published a book entitled *The Art of Decorative Design*, and fourteen years later went to Japan on a government mission. After he had returned laden with samples of many varieties of the arts of that country he wrote a book on Japan. In it he stated that he had come back with 1,000 photographs, numerous coloured drawings and that he had visited sixty-eight potteries: 'I also bought specimens of work from most of the factories visited.'

From the foregoing it is likely that he was strongly influenced by seeing so much, and *japonaiserie* was to be apparent in his work from then onward. A typical Dresser-Clutha vase is shown in Plate 76, where the studiedly casual appearance with its spiralling forms and 'faults' was perhaps the result of having seen some of the stoneware used by the Japanese in their tea ceremony. Webb's made a rather similar type of glass which they named 'Old Roman'.

Equally individualistic, but completely different in conception from Clutha, is the set of jug and tumblers in Plate 77. It was made to Dresser's design, and as the mounts bear the London date-letter for 1882 they pre-date his work for Couper's and perhaps also his Japanese visit. While the tumblers are more or less conventional in looks, the jug would be difficult to date at a glance and few people would guess that it had been made during Victoria's reign. As has been shown, almost everything else of the period was shaped or coloured or decorated almost to the point of the grotesque, but this group of pieces is quite different. It is not a completely isolated example, but it shows, as do some comparable articles, that a complete change in style was beginning to take place.

Contemporaneous comment on what was fashionable at the very close of the century was penned by Rosamund Marriott Watson, who contributed a series of articles on decoration to the *Pall Mall Gazette*. In 1897, they were reprinted in book form. The author deplores the garish colours and poor design of so much of the Venetian-style glass of the day, shows disapproval of engraved glass flower vases, and refers with scorn to 'the inane little specimen glass'. On the other hand, she welcomes some recently-introduced 'replicas of antique glass vases, urns and tear-vessels . . . some tapering and slim-necked, others with a kind of archaic beauty of outline not to be despised'.

Not least, the writer enthuses, perhaps rather unexpectedly, over traditional cut wares: 'The modern replicas of the old diamond-cut glass could scarce be better of their kind; there is a cheerful and abiding charm about the sparkling solidity of an array of these; a quality that inspires confidence, that invites esteem without appealing too strongly to the imagination.' The wheel, it seems, has turned full circle in the course of sixty or so years.

6
Nailsea-type glass

Throughout the nineteenth century a distinctive variety of glassware was produced to which the generic name 'Nailsea' has become attached. Some examples were summarily-finished utilitarian items of green glass splashed with opaque white, in the form of such articles as jugs, cups and flagons, made for local sale at cheap rates. Others were probably made in the glasshouses as spare-time amusements or to test skill, and were later displayed on the mantelshelves of the makers' families or on those of their friends. These objects included some for domestic use, as well as less practical trivialities like walking-sticks, hats and drum-sticks; all of them partly coloured with internal threads or external splashes.

The oft-repeated tale is that wares of both kinds originated at Nailsea, about ten miles from Bristol, where someone realized that articles made from common sheet or bottle glass could be sold at lower prices than those made from flint glass because the duty on the former was less. However, the Nailsea source, except in the case of a small number of specimens, receives little support from modern authorities, but the use of the name persists. A small quantity of such wares may have come from Nailsea in the course of the century as a by-product in the making of Crown glass and bottles, as it was not unusual for glasshouses of the kind to make as a side line sturdy articles like cloches, milk-pans and rolling-pins. Equally, it is quite certain that exactly similar goods were made during the same period at many other glasshouses.

Although it is known that bottles were made for a time at Nailsea, the principal output was sheet glass for windows. In 1831 it was noted that: 'In this parish are extensive coal-works, and a manufactory for crown glass upon a very large scale, which together give employment to a great portion of the inhabitants.' Probably by that date the bottle-making had ceased, and sheet glass only was being produced.

There are differences in the composition and appearance of green-tinted Crown glass and bottle glass and flint (or lead) glass, and a lack of recognition of the distinctions has led to erroneous attributions. Sir Hugh Chance, a descendant of William Chance who became a partner in the Nailsea concern in 1793, is himself a glass-maker of renown. In 1967 he wrote on the subject of his ancestor's activities, and alluding to the flint glass articles that have been, and all too often still are, labelled as Nailsea, stated: '... if the collector wishes to put a name to such items he can choose between "Bristol" and "Stourbridge", according to his taste! But he will definitely be wrong if he assigns them to the Nailsea works.'

Legend has it that some houses at Nailsea named 'French Rank' were the homes of some French glass-makers who came to England, and were responsible for many of the factory's more colourful productions. The cottages, which have been demolished, existed, but the rest of the story is less likely to be authentic. A Frenchman named Louis Amede worked there in an unspecified capacity, and 'three glass flatteners called Desguin', from the same country, all of whom were there in the 1860s, but there is no local record of others of their nationality or of any other immigrants being employed. It is possible that the story of foreign workers owes its origin to the bizarre appearance of many of the brightly coloured and striped so-called Nailsea pieces.

Some of the wares are technically distant cousins of old Venetian articles, many of which were no less fanciful in appearance. This may perhaps be because the English glass-makers had acquired a knowledge of the foreign examples, but it is much more likely to be because of a similarity in the properties of the metal used at both places and the universal methods of manufacture.

The direct inspiration of many of the objects was to be found in the trade processions that took place annually; displays at which the glass-makers advertised their solidarity as workers at the same time as they demonstrated their skill. The processions were sometimes reported at some length in newspapers, and some of the accounts have been frequently reprinted and referred to, notably those that took place in Bristol in 1738 and in Newcastle upon Tyne in 1823.

A less-publicized display of the same kind was held at Plymouth, Devon, a town not normally associated with glass-making, but possessing a manufactory at the time that has so far eluded research to discover further details. The newspaper report refers to celebrations of the coronation of Queen Victoria in 1838, and although lengthy is worth reproducing.

After stating that the workers from the glasshouse went in procession through the three adjoining towns of Plymouth, Devonport and Stonehouse, the reporter described the composition of the cavalcade:

A band of musicians; a banner, bearing on the one side a representation of the exterior, and on the other the interior, of the Glass-House at Millbay; guards on horseback, bearing battle-axes made of twisted and cut glass; a royal crown of massive cut glass, ornamented with bead work, and imitation jewels of cut glass, placed on a cushion of crimson velvet, borne by a glass-maker; two boys bearing glass wands, surmounted by glass doves; a radiant star of richly cut glass, borne by a glass-worker, supported on right and left by boys bearing glass wands, surmounted by garlands of cut glass; a large globe of flint glass, threaded with pearl-coloured semi-transparent enamel, borne by a glass-worker, and supported on the right and left by boys bearing glass wands, surmounted by miniature crowns of cut glass; a glass barrel, surmounted by a cut glass drinking vessel and a crown, the barrel ornamented with stripes of milk-white enamel, borne by a glass-worker, and supported on the right and left by boys bearing glass wands, surmounted by wreaths; a cut glass basket, richly ornamented and filled with flowers . . .; a crown and sceptre, of richly cut glass . . .; a glass globe, ornamented and supported as before; decanters and wine glasses, of superior festoon patterns, richly cut, and placed on a crimson velvet cushion, borne by a glass-worker, and supported by boys bearing ornamental wands. The men wore glass hats, which had a very imposing effect – a novelty never witnessed in Plymouth before.

From the foregoing, it is not difficult to imagine that the craftsmen took advantage of their spare time and any surplus molten glass to make similar articles for themselves. Not improbably they looked upon the pieces displayed in public as perquisites and took them home. In time such objects found their way to curio shops, before long a demand arose for more and they became part of the normal daily output. Harry J. Powell wrote of them in 1923, after a lifetime's experience in the glass industry: '... known as "friggers" [they] may be seen as chimney-piece ornaments in glass-blowers' homes in every glass-making district. In the Bristol district these by-products were exploited by dealers and became for a time staple products. They were widely distributed, and copies are still made in many districts and sold as antiques.'

The various articles changed so little in their general appearance from the time when they were first made that it is difficult to date them accurately. The usual criterion of style is seldom of assistance, the presence or absence of a pontil-mark is no guide at all and, as with other glassware, it is not difficult to falsify wear-and-tear to give a spurious indication of age. Even with pieces that were not made deliberately for retailing, however, the old-time craftsmen took more trouble than their successors. Superior workmanship can sometimes be detected by an experienced collector, and the colours used, singly or in combination, can often provide a clue.

Once upon a time, it might have been possible to attribute an example to the region in which it was located; it is tempting to say that a piece found in the Nailsea area was made there. Several decades ago, before the invention of the motor-car, travel was comparatively difficult, especially in districts not served by railways. Life was then incomparably less hectic than it has since become, so that furniture, china and glass and other chattels were likely to remain undisturbed from the day they were acquired. If disposed of, they would be sold in the immediate locality and probably not travel many miles from their first home. It was possible to be fairly certain that if a manufactory had existed at some time in an area, its products would be found thereabouts. For example, a number of wine and other glasses with distinctive horizontal ribbing on their bowls were found in the 1890s in the region of King's Lynn. There had been a glasshouse in the town in the previous century, so it was not unreasonably assumed that these pieces had come from it. The attribution remains unshaken to the present day. Nowadays, antiques of all kinds have travelled so far and so often from their original homes that their present locations are very seldom of value in attributing origins.

Strictly speaking, friggers were the work of glass-men and were made within the walls of the glasshouses in which they were employed. Another range of fanciful objects was made in the open streets and at markets and fairs, by men who used a type of glass that melted in the comparatively low temperature of a lamp-flame. They set up their stands wherever an audience was likely to form; one of them advertised as long ago as 1702 that he 'in the presence of all spectators maketh beasts, birds, fowls, images, figures of men and women which he bloweth in all colours of glass'.

The most spectacular of the productions were the models of fountains and sailing-ships, the latter often complete with members of the crew in the rigging. Such elaborate pieces could not have been made in the space of the few minutes it would have taken to complete more commonplace lamp-made items. Probably they were made to order, or perhaps displayed to the public as proof of the skill of their makers. In an undated announcement, two men named Davis and Johnson stated that they were 'the only glass ship builders travelling the Kingdom'.

Messrs Davis and Johnson helpfully appended a list of some of their output, prefaced by the boast that 'they will blow any article while the company are present'. Mr Johnson's role in the partnership is not made clear, as it would seem that the other man did the work. The list reads: 'Mr. Davis makes a variety of ornaments for sale such as feathers, pens, plain and ornamental necklaces, ships, flowers and pipes, tobacco stoppers, cigar tubes, microscopes, spirit levels, trees, birds and birds' nests, seals with a variety of other articles too numerous to insert.'

These itinerants, and many others who followed in their footsteps, were no less versatile than the men working in glasshouses. Old lamp-made articles are uncommon, as they were mostly small in size and especially fragile. Like the Nailsea-type wares they are often difficult to date, have been copied in the present century and must usually be admired for the virtuosity they exhibit rather than their age.

Appendix: Victorian glass manufacture and decoration

Glass is made by melting silica in a furnace, but in normal practice this requires too high a temperature and a flux is added to facilitate the process. The silica employed is sand, flint or quartz, and the flux is an alkali varying between soda and potash according to availability and local practice. It may be accounted a wonder of nature that such apparently unpromising ingredients should combine to form a material that has given service and pleasure to mankind for untold hundreds of years.

By the beginning of the nineteenth century good English domestic glassware was made from a mixture of fine sand, with potash as the alkaline flux and lead oxide to provide stability and an improved appearance. Everyday articles were composed of sand, lime and soda, which gave a product no less durable than the other but lacking its perfect clarity and much of its sparkle. In both instances, impurities in the form of iron, which could not be removed from the silica, resulted in a green tint, but this could be neutralized by the addition of a small quantity of manganese.

Whichever type of glass was to be made, the ingredients were purified so far as was possible at the time, and proportioned one to another according to the recipe followed. The prepared mixture was known as the 'batch', and when fully combined was shovelled into a large baked-clay crucible of special shape, with a mouth to one side at the top: a 'pot'. The pot was already in place within the furnace, with its opening facing outwards for due access to its contents, and the heat was raised gradually to about 1,400–1,500°C. Up to 48 hours could elapse before the contents of the pots were in the correct state for use by the glass-makers.

It was found a long time ago that glass in its melted and syrup-like state had an affinity with iron, and the craftsman was able to remove what he required from the pot by dipping into it an iron rod. The lump of molten glass was a 'gather' and he gathered it on the end of a 'pontil', which was a simple rod, or on a blowing-iron, according to the job to be performed. With the aid of the latter, a hollow rod, he could blow a globe of glass in a manner similar to that of a child blowing a soap-bubble, while the pontil was used in handling the blown and partly-finished article. This was performed by taking up a small gather on the end of the pontil and sticking it to the article; once the latter was held on the pontil, the blowing-iron, which had played its part and was no longer required, could be broken away. Any further shaping and finishing were then carried out, the pontil finally being removed and leaving a scar known as a pontil-mark where it had been attached. The rough mark was usually left untouched on pieces made prior to about the year 1800, but from then onwards an increasing proportion had all trace of the mark ground away and the area polished. The presence or absence of a pontil-mark is not neccssarily an indication of age, as it is not unknown for it to have been left intact in order to give a false appearance of antiquity to a fake.

In the execution of hand-made or 'free-blown' ware the glass-makers worked in groups, each group being known as a 'chair' or 'shop'. A chair varied in its composition, but one with a team of five would have included the undermentioned:

Gaffer: principal glass-blower and in charge of the shop. The term 'gaffer' is often applied in other trades to a foreman or manager.
Servitor: chief assistant to the gaffer.
Footmaker: maker of subsidiary parts of an article, such as the foot of a wine glass, to be attached by the servitor.
Taker in: boy who carried finished articles to the leer for annealing.

The number of men and boys in a shop varied according to the size of the establishment where they worked, and the type of goods being made. Wine glass making, for example, might have required a team of four: gaffer, servitor, footmaker and taker in.

In practice, the craftsman dipped his blowing-iron into the pot and gathered on it a quantity of glass ('metal'), but often a succession of gathers was needed before he had enough for the work to be done. He next rolled the mass on a flat block of iron, known as a 'marver', so as to shape roughly the hot glass which at that stage was known as a 'paraison'. The paraison could be re-heated at the furnace-mouth or at an opening in a smaller subsidiary furnace known as a 'glory hole'. It was then blown, further blown and fashioned to requirements with the aid of cutting-shears, pincers and tools.

The outer surfaces of an article cool more quickly from contact with the air than do the areas within the walls, and if no action was taken to correct this the article would be unstable. In this condition it might shatter unexpectedly as a result of casual handling or from any other cause. The process of annealing relieved the stresses, by means of very slow cooling from melting heat down to normal. For the purpose, the article was placed in a 'leer' (or 'lehr'), in which the temperature was gradually lowered, and it then became serviceable.

Terms that were commonly employed in connection with glass-making and decorating include those which follow below. Among them may be noticed a number of foreign ones which can be traced back to the days when the Venetian Republic was the centre of the European glass industry. For ease of reference a number of the terms mentioned in the preceding paragraphs are included in an expanded form.

Annealing The slow cooling of finished glass articles is essential in order to remove internal stresses that might otherwise be acquired. Objects that have not been annealed would be liable to shatter without warning (see **Leer**).

Batch The ingredients of glass made ready for melting.

Blowing-iron An iron tube ranging in diameter from ½ in to 1½ in (1·3–3·8 cm), and in length from about 3 ft (91·5 cm) upwards according to the articles it was required to form.

Bohemian glass Bohemia now forms part of Czechoslovakia and has long been a centre of glass-making. In the nineteenth century the industry exported large quantities of its products to England. The majority was coloured, much of it decorated with cutting, painting and gilding, and in many instances difficult to distinguish from imitations made at Stourbridge and elsewhere. For some of their best glass the Bohemian makers used a recipe with 71 per cent silica, 12 per cent potash, 10 per cent lime and a trace of manganese. Another maker, near Gratzen, had his ware subjected to analysis and it was found to contain nearly 79 per cent silica, 12 per cent soda and 5 per cent of both soda and lime. No doubt each glasshouse had its own variation.

Broad glass Sheet glass made by the Broad or Lorraine process was used for windows as an alternative to glass made by the Crown method. The manufacture of the panes, each 49 in (1·245 m) in length, for the Great Exhibition building, was described as follows: 'A quantity of molten glass having been collected on the extremity of the iron blower, is distended first into a spherical form; it is then heated in the furnace, and the glowing mass is swung round by the workman, who stands on the edge of a pit, until it becomes elongated to the required extent. The cylinder thus formed is then cut off at both ends, is cut [lengthwise] through the middle, placed in a flattening furnace, where it is spread out upon a slab quite flat. After being annealed the pane is completed.'

Cameo glass The Romans used cased glass, carved in the manner of stone and shell cameos, of which the most famous surviving example is the Portland vase in the British Museum. The art was revived at Stourbridge by

John Northwood in the 1870s. In most instances a coloured glass was cased with white, the latter being cut away to form a decorative pattern. The carving was assisted by first etching out the larger unwanted areas, and then the worker painstakingly chiselled away at the details with the aid of steel instruments. Delicate gradations of light and shade could be achieved, and the successful results were, and still are, looked upon as triumphs of craftsmanship.

Cameo incrustation Cameo incrustations are, literally, cameos encrusted in glass. They were produced in Paris in the late eighteenth century, and patented in London in 1819 by Apsley Pellatt of the Falcon glassworks. He named his version 'Crystallo Ceramie'. The process involved the enclosing of a moulded porcellaneous cameo within a covering of glass. The maker formed an open-ended 'cup' into which the cameo was placed; then, instead of blowing down the iron, suction caused the glass to collapse and completely cover the cameo on all sides. The finished object displays the cameo with an attractive silvery appearance. Pellatt himself wrote that 'these incrustations require very careful annealing', no doubt because of the disparity between the materials involved, and manufacturing losses were probably high.

Cane The name given to patterned glass rods, of which slices were used to form the patterns in glass paperweights. The canes were assembled from lengths of coloured glass fused together, and then stretched until they were of the required diameter.

Casing This is covering a vessel made of one glass with an outer coating of another colour. Andrew Ure wrote in 1853: 'Crystal vessels have been made recently of which the inner surface is colourless, and all the external facets coloured. Such works are easily executed. The end of the blowing-rod must be dipped first in the pot containing colourless glass, to form a bulb of a certain size, which being cooled a little is then dipped for an instant into the pot of coloured glass. The two layers are associated without intermixture; and when the article is finished in its form, it is white within and coloured without. Fluted lines somewhat deeply cut, pass through the coloured coat, and enter the colourless one; so that when they cross, their ends alone are coloured.' All kinds of articles were cased in one or more colours, the range including vases, paperweights and lustres. The basis of cameo glass was a cased vessel.

Casting see **Plate glass.**

Chair This was the name given to a group of craftsmen who worked as a team. Alternatively it applied to a special type of seat without a back, but with side-arms extended at back and front on which the blowing-iron could be rolled with a vessel affixed to the iron. It not only enabled the craftsman to work on the article, but the motion prevented the semi-molten form from collapsing.

Colours Finely-ground metal oxides were the basis of most of the colours in which glass is found. Pale greens and brown were usually a result of impurities in the form of iron naturally in the sand, and this could be neutralized, or (decolourized) by the addition of a small amount of manganese. Popular colours were obtained by adding suitable amounts of oxides or other substances as follows:

Amethyst: manganese and cobalt.
Black: Manganese and iron.
Blue: copper or cobalt.
Green: iron; and iron and copper.
Green-yellow: uranium, giving the type of opalescent yellow glass named 'Vaseline' glass because of its resemblance in colour to the well-known petroleum jelly.
Red (ruby): gold chloride made by dissolving pure gold in a mixture of hydrochloric and nitric acids; or copper oxide. Use of either produced a colourless glass that developed its ruby-red or cranberry tint on being re-heated.
White: bone ash (calcium phosphate), the white powder resulting from the burning of animals' bones; or tin oxide; or arsenic. Use of any one of these gave an opaque white glass, a milk glass or a semi-transparent opal glass.

Crimping mould A simple appliance, made from rods of wood or metal radiating from a central core, for forming an evenly-spaced crimping at the mouths of vases and other vessels. The crimper was pressed on to the molten top of the article.

Crown glass The Normandy or Crown process was employed for making ordinary sheet glass for windows. A large bubble was blown and opposite the point of contact with the blowing-iron a pontil was attached by a small lump of molten glass. The iron was broken away to leave a hole, and with the hole facing the furnace mouth the pontil was rotated rapidly. At a certain point the bubble suddenly collapsed to form a flat disc measuring up to about 5 ft (1·525 m) in diameter and weighing some 9 lb. After the pontil had been broken away, the disc was annealed for approximately 24 hours and then flat pieces were cut from it leaving a bulging bull's eye where the pontil had been. The bull's eye is sometimes seen in use as a decorative window, being much favoured for 'Tudor tea shoppes'. Crown glass panes were seldom, if ever, perfectly flat, the process resulting in a surface with curves and ripples. It had the advantage of a bright finish that required neither grinding nor polishing, thereby saving labour and expense.

Crystal A term used to describe lead glass or close imitations of it, all of them attempting to simulate natural rock crystal.

Crystallo ceramie See **Cameo incrustation.**

Cullet This was broken and discarded glass, either from the glasshouse or bought from those who collected it in towns and villages. It was added to the batch and had the effect of assisting melting. Cullet also cost less than the ingredients for which it was substituted.

Cutting The decoration of glass by means of cut ornament was introduced into England from Germany during the first quarter of the eighteenth century. It duly became popular, and the public continued to favour it into the early years of Victoria's reign. After the removal of the glass duty in 1845 cutting was largely supplanted by colour, but it never went entirely out of favour and in one style or another was to be found on glassware throughout the nineteenth century. A description of a cutting workshop was printed by Andrew Ure in 1853, and was applicable, by and large, during the ensuing fifty years. Ure wrote that 'the cutting shop should be a spacious long apartment, furnished with numerous skylights, having the grinding and polishing lathes arranged right under them, which are set in motion by a steam-engine or water-wheel at one end of the building'. The operation was performed by holding the article against a wheel made of iron, sandstone, tin, copper or wood, according to the task being undertaken. There was a constant drip of abrasive and water or polishing medium and water on to the wheels, depending on whether cutting or polishing was being undertaken. For the latter, putty – a mixture of red lead and tin oxide – was used. However, this was injurious to health, and at the end of the century it was reported that the average life-span of those working with it was no more than fifty-five years.

Engraving Glass-engraving was executed using wheels fed with abrasive and water as in cutting. Small diameter wheels were employed so as to produce a delicate effect, and greater skills were called for. According to John Northwood, sr, the wheel was turned by a treadle controlled by the engraver, the depth of cut being limited by the modest power available. In the 1880s a variation known as 'rock crystal engraving' was introduced at

Stourbridge, this work resembling cutting and with the hollows polished. A power-driven lathe was used for its execution.

Etching Glass was etched with hydrofluoric acid, the desired pattern being scratched through a coating of waxy varnish with which the article had been covered. The patterns were sometimes drawn by hand, but could also be executed by a machine using templates. These were made of tinfoil, but if popular and much employed would have been of copper or brass. Such a machine was devised by John Northwood, who first put it to use in 1861. Soon afterwards, he devised another machine for cutting geometrical designs, like the Greek Key or endless interlaced circles, which remained popular for many decades.

Fire Polish To give an article a brilliant surface while removing blemishes, it was held at the furnace-mouth so that the surface just melted. Fire-polishing was used for finishing press-moulded goods, on which it removed or lessened mould marks and surface roughnesses, and for crown glass.

Flashing The word flashing has two meanings in glass-making. When Crown glass was being spun at the mouth of the furnace it suddenly, 'in a flash', flattened from a bubble into a flat disc. The term also applied to the covering of a clear glass article with a thin coating of coloured glass, so that the article remained transparent. Some of the colours would have been too dark if used in the solid.

Flint glass See **Lead glass**.

Friggers According to W. A. Thorpe a frigger was 'an experimental or apprentice piece'. In modern times the term has been stretched in meaning to include much that was produced commercially in the shape of glass rolling-pins, hand-bells, witch-balls, walking-sticks and what are sometimes termed 'cottage antiques', whether old or not. More accurately, the word 'frigger' should be applied to articles made by glass-workers for the amusement of themselves, their families and friends, but it is obviously impossible to decide in most instances if a particular example is in this category or not.

Furnace The glasshouse in use during the nineteenth century was a tall, conical brick structure standing between 60 and 100 ft (18·29–30·48 m) in height. Within, in the centre, was the furnace over which stood the pots. They were encircled by a wall pierced with working-holes through which the contents of the pots could be reached.

Gadget The gadget was a rod fitted at the end with a spring grip to hold an object during making. Use of the gadget enabled the finished work to be easily released, and it left no marks where it had been applied. It replaced the pontil in making wine glasses and other footed articles.

Glasshouse See **Furnace**.

Glory-hole A working-hole in a furnace at which articles could be re-heated during manufacture. It has been suggested that it acquired its name because it was hot and hell-like within, and gave the glass-maker a vision of his future existence.

Ice glass The so-called ice glass originated in Venice in the sixteenth century and was revived by Apsley Pellatt, Bacchus, and perhaps others, in about 1850. It gave articles the appearance of being made of cracked ice, and could be produced by two ingenious methods. The finished object could be plunged briefly into water, while itself still hot and un-annealed, and then re-heated to fuse the cracks that had been formed. Alternatively, molten glass could be rolled to pick up fragments, thus achieving a comparable effect.

Latticinio *Latticinio* or *latticino* is clear glass in which is embedded a pattern of threads of opaque white, and sometimes coloured, glass. It was made by placing rods of the white or colour round the evenly-ridged interior of a mould, and then blowing a bubble of clear glass into it. The rods adhered to the bubble, were marvered into it, and then manipulated to form a pattern. The term is applied to Venetian glass and to imitations of it.

Lead glass Lead or flint glass was invented in about 1676 by George Ravenscroft, an Englishman, who had been engaged by the Glassmakers' Company, of London, to find a replacement for the large quantities of glass then being imported into England from Venice and elsewhere. He found that by adding lead oxide (red lead) to the batch, he not only produced a glass equal to the imported but one that was better – more brilliant in appearance, and with what has been described in apt words by W. B. Honey as 'a light-dispersing character that gave it a natural interior fire'. At first the silica employed was in the form of English flints, burnt and reduced to powder, hence the name of flint glass, but this ingredient was soon replaced by sand. The original name, flint glass, continued to be used, but present practice is to refer to it as lead glass. In addition to its distinctive appearance, it is found that glass containing lead oxide is noticeably heavier in the hand than other varieties.

A recipe for flint glass published by Apsley Pellatt in 1849 consisted of:

Carbonate of potash	1 cwt (about 50 kg)
Red lead or litharge	2 cwt

> Sand, washed and burnt 3 cwt
> Saltpetre 14–28 lb
> Oxide of manganese 4–12 oz (340 g)

Another, of 1853, listed:

> Fine sand 50·5 parts
> Litharge 27·2 parts
> Refined pearl ashes 17·5 parts
>   (carbonate of potash with 5 per cent water)
> Nitre 4·8 parts

To these quantities from 30 to 50 parts of broken glass or cullet are added; with about a two-thousandth part of manganese and a three-thousandth part of arsenic.

As soon as Ravenscroft had perfected his new glass it quickly became standard in most English glasshouses, and remains in production to the present day. The two recipes quoted above are only random examples of the many that have been tried from time to time, all varying to a greater or lesser degree but all containing a good proportion of lead oxide. It is true to say that almost every glasshouse had its own preferred recipe, each varying in some particular from another, but basically following in the footsteps of George Ravenscroft.

Ravenscroft's lead glass was accepted as being an improvement on the Venetian product. This was undeniable as regards its appearance, but it was quickly found that in working it was also different. The imported glass had soda as its alkali, which made the molten material slow to cool and enabled the craftsman to manipulate articles into elaborate forms. On the other hand, the comparatively fast-cooling lead glass did not permit such fancies, except with difficulty, and the result was that English articles were, on the whole, of much more severe appearance. Thus, the new recipe played an important part in the creation of a truly English style in glassware, forcing the makers to cease imitating imported wares and making them concentrate on shapes and ornament consistent with the characteristics of the metal (see **Crystal**).

Lead oxide Lead oxide is the constituent in lead glass that gives it its intrinsic merits (see **Lead glass**).

Leer Newly-made wares were annealed in the leer or lehr. A description of those in use in the early 1850s states that in effect they were large and long flues, each with a fire at one end and a chimney at the other: 'On the floor of the vault, large iron trays are laid and hooked to each other in a series, which are drawn from the fire end towards the other by a chain, wound about a cylinder by a winch-handle projecting through the side. The flint-glass articles are placed in their hot state into the tray next the fire, which is moved onwards to a cooler station whenever it is filled, and an empty tray set in its place. Thus, in the course of about 20 hours the glass advances to the cool end thoroughly annealed.'

Manganese Manganese oxide, sometimes referred to as 'glass-maker's soap' was added in a very small quantity to decolourize a batch. It had the effect of neutralizing the brown or green tints due to the presence of iron. If too much manganese was used the glass was made black, amethyst or pink according to the amount put in. Wares containing manganese acquire a bright purple hue with exposure to the rays of the sun.

Marver A flat slab, usually of iron, on which the molten glass on the end of the blowing-iron was rolled to give it its initial shape prior to blowing.

Metal Glass, whether hot and molten or cold and hard.

Millefiori An Italian word meaning 'thousand flowers', used to describe glass that appears to be patterned with innumerable miniature flower-heads. In fact, they are slices of coloured cane, which were either fused together to form the walls of a vessel or were arranged in the interior of a paperweight. Millefiori glass was made by the Romans, and its best-known revival took place in France where they made the paperweights showing it to great advantage.

Moulding Glass could be ornamented by blowing it into a mould. The mould, usually made of metal, was patterned in the interior in the reverse manner to the finished effect: i.e. the parts to appear raised were cut in intaglio, and the depressions were in relief. The mould was often hinged so that a vessel could be withdrawn without difficulty or damage after it had been blown. Frequently, a moulded object was further enlarged by blowing after it had been taken from the mould, the pattern expanding along with whatever it ornamented. The difference between blown-moulding and press-moulding is that the former bears the pattern in reverse in the interior of the article. A press-moulded specimen shows on its inner surface only the smooth impression of the plunger.

Paraison The molten glass gathered from the pot on the end of the blowing-iron following its initial shaping on the marver.

Pillar-moulding A decorative pattern of heavy ribs on the exterior of an article. Pillar-moulding was used, like so many other techniques, by the

Romans, and their manner of execution has been hotly debated. Apsley Pellat wrote about it in 1849 and described an ingenious way of achieving such an effect. He advocated taking a gather of glass, and when it had cooled slightly covering it with a fresh gather. Blowing the two into a mould resulted in the outer gather acquiring the pattern, while the less plastic inner gather remained more or less even-surfaced.

Pincering Ornament formed with the aid of a tool somewhat like a carpenter's pincers. The drops hanging from chandeliers, candelabra and other objects could be formed with the aid of a specially shaped pair of pincers.

Plate glass Thick sheet glass with a flat surface which could be made in two ways: by the Broad process or by casting. The latter was a French process until 1773, when The British Cast Plate Manufacturers, with factories at Southwark, London, and Ravenhead, near St Helens, Lancashire, were incorporated. The plates were cast on large flat tables with raised edges adjustable for size, to which the molten metal was brought in large iron containers. These were tipped when over the tables, the contents poured out and rollers used to spread it evenly. The sheets were then annealed and polished to remove imperfections. Sheets made by the Broad process were limited in size, mostly by the strength of the blower's lungs, whereas cast plates could be made considerably larger.

Polishing See **Cutting**.

Pontil A plain iron rod, sometimes called a punty or pontee, used for holding an article during manufacture. It was tipped with a small blob of molten glass for the purpose, and when its work was completed it was broken away. The scar remaining is known as the pontil-mark, and is commonly found on most eighteenth-century glassware. It is less frequently seen on pieces made from the turn of the century onwards, as it became increasingly the practice to grind away the mark and polish the area. Alternatively, a gadget was used for holding a vessel of suitable shape (see **Gadget**).

Pontil-mark See **Pontil**.

Press-moulding W. C. Aitken wrote the following explanatory note printed in the glass section of the Great Exhibition *Catalogue*: 'By pressing is meant the mode of producing ornamentation on glass in moulds by pressure, and is effected by a press, plunger, and metal-mould, corresponding in internal shape to the article to be produced. The workman receives from a servitor a melted mass of glass, of which he drops a quantity into the mould, and disconnects it from the rod by cutting it off with a pair of scissors; the mould with the melted glass is then placed under the plunger, it is screwed down, which forces the glass into every marking. Minute fissures or cracks which are observable on the surface are removed by again heating the object made, which is now attached to a 'punty', and causing it to revolve while the workman holds it against a piece of timber, the heat of which, when red, speedily fuses the whole of the exterior of the glass article to a uniform surface.'

As the century progressed the process was improved, and in the 1880s it was reported that a man working a normal eight-hour shift (actually only seven hours, as an hour was allowed for mealtimes) could turn out between 1,000 and 1,200 tumblers.

Procellas A glass-making tool resembling a large pair of sugar-tongs, used for widening the mouth of a vessel or other article during manufacture. They were made of iron with pear-wood ends where they came in contact with the glass, and are sometimes referred to as pucellas.

Quilted glass A modern name for articles decorated with an all-over diamond pattern beneath the surface (see **Trapped air**).

Satin glass Glass with a dull, silky surface, popular in the 1880s. The finish was obtained by immersing the article in a bath of acid.

Shears A scissors-like tool with which molten glass was cut. With it the worker could trim an article, and was also able to regulate the amount of material required for a particular purpose (see **Press-moulding**).

Soda glass See **Bohemian glass.**

Sulphide See **Cameo-incrustation.**

Trapped air If a vessel was moulded on the exterior with, say, a diamond pattern and this was then cased, the air in the moulded channels would be trapped inside. The effect would be scarcely visible but attractive, with a resemblance to quilting, by which name it is sometimes known today. Airlock or air-trapped patterns were popular in the 1880s, when vases and other articles were made of opaque glass cased in a tinted one, the finished piece usually being given a satin finish.

Venetian glass The Venetians were internationally famous for their skill in glass-making from as early as the fourteenth century. The industry became located on the island of Murano, where fires from the furnaces would not imperil buildings in the nearby city. Workers were strictly forbidden to leave the country, and the government controlled all aspects of glass-making in order to preserve the valuable monopoly. In the end, Venetians risked their lives by travelling to other countries where they established rival glasshouses, and it can occasionally be difficult, if not impossible, to distinguish the products of Antwerp and elsewhere from those of Venice.

The Venetian metal was made from a silica in the form of quartz pebbles from river beds, with a mixture of soda and lime as the flux. The result was a slow-cooling glass that allowed time for the craftsman to execute the typical pincering and other manipulation. Equally characteristic are vessels with thin walls, light weight, and a resemblance to dull-surfaced horn rather than to clear shining glass. Probably the best known of all old Venetian wares are those with fine threads, usually opaque white but sometimes coloured, embedded in the clear glass and skilfully formed into lace-like patterns. These and other pieces were closely imitated during the eighteenth and nineteenth centuries.

Bibliography

Yolande Amic, *L'Opaline Française au XIX siècle* (Paris, 1952).
L. M. Angus-Butterworth, *British Table and Ornamental Glass* (1956).
Art-Journal Illustrated Catalogue of the Industry of All Nations (1851).
Art-Journal Illustrated Catalogue of the International Exhibition (1862).
Geoffrey W. Beard, *Nineteenth Century Cameo Glass* (Newport, Mon., 1956).
Shirley Bury, 'Felix Summerly's Art Manufactures', *Apollo*, January, 1967.
Sir Hugh Chance, 'Records and the Nailsea Glassworks', *The Connoisseur*, July, 1967.
R. W. Douglas and S. Frank, *A History of Glassmaking* (1972).
C. L. Eastlake, *Hints on Household Taste* (1868).
Paul Gardner, *The Glass of Frederick Carder* (New York, 1971).
Geoffrey A. Godden, *Antique China and Glass under £5* (1966).
Montague J. Guest (ed.), *Lady Charlotte Schreiber's Journals*, 2 vols (1911).
D. R. Guttery, *From Broad-Glass to Cut Crystal* (1956).
H. J. Haden, *Notes on the Stourbridge Glass Trade* (Dudley, 1949).
Helga Hilschenz, *Das Glas des Jugendstils* (Munich, 1973).
Paul Hollister, Jr, *The Encyclopaedia of Glass Paperweights* (New York, 1969).
W. B. Honey, *Glass* (1946).
Mrs Loftie, *The Dining Room* (1878).
Henry Mayhew, *London Labour and the London Poor*, 3 vols (1851–64).
R. G. Newton, 'Metallic Gold and Ruby Glass', *Journal of Glass Studies*, XIII, 1970.
John Northwood II, *John Northwood* (Stourbridge, 1958).
Official Descriptive and Illustrated Catalogue of the Great Exhibition, 3 vols (1851) and supplementary vol. [1853].
Betty O'Looney, *Victorian Glass* (Victoria and Albert Museum, 1972).
Emma Papert, *The Illustrated Guide to American Glass* (New York, 1972).
Apsley Pellatt, *Curiosities of Glass Making* (1849).
Harry J. Powell, *Glass-Making in England* (Cambridge, 1923).
Gerald Reitlinger, *The Economics of Taste*, Vol. II (1963).
A. C. Revi, *Nineteenth Century Glass* (New York, 1959).
A. W. M. Stirling, *The Richmond Papers* (1926).
J. Tallis and Co., *Tallis's History and Description of the Great Exhibition*, 8 vols (1851).
W. A. Thorpe, *A History of English and Irish Glass*, 2 vols (1929).
John Timbs, *The Year Book of Facts in the Great Exhibition* (1851).

Andrew Ure, *A Dictionary of Arts, Manufactures and Mines*, 2 vols (1853).
Keith Vincent, *Nailsea Glass* (Newton Abbot, 1975).
Hugh Wakefield, *19th Century British Glass* (1961).
Rosamund Marriott Watson, *The Art of the House* (1897).
Geoffrey Wills, *Antique Glass* (1970).
Sir Henry Trueman Wood, *A History of the Royal Society of Arts* (1913).

Index

Acanthus leaves, depiction of, 52–3
Adam, Robert, 1–2
Ailsa Jug, 28 and Pl. 26
Aitken, W. C., 82
Alabaster, glass resembling, 16
Albert, Prince Consort, 11, 18, 27, 47, Pl. 64
Ale glasses *see* Glasses
Alexandra Palace, engraving of, Pl. 24
Amber (colour), glass tinted with, 16, 64, Pls. 58, 73
Amede, Louis, 68
Amethyst (colour), glass tinted with, 9, 76, 81
Amphora, Pl. 25
Andrew Ker & Co., Manchester, Pl. 33
Annagelb, 7, 9
Annagrün, 7, 9
Annealing, 73, 74
Apsley Pellatt & Co., 6, 16–17, 28, Pl. 25
Aqua regia, in production of ruby glass, 51
Arsenic, 80
Art Journal, 28, 35
Art of Decorative Design, The, C. Dresser, 65–6
Authentication
   and dating, 7, 68, 70, 71
   of Nailsea glass, 68, 70
   of Venetian glass, 35–6
   of work of itinerant glass-makers, 71

Baccarat, glass works at, 24
Bacchus *see* George Bacchus and Sons
Bagot, Lady Mary, 21
Barnard, Jabez, 38
Basins, sugar, cream, 4, 16, 21, 25, 51, Pl. 71
Baskets, Pls. 45, 70
Batch, defined, 72, 74

Bee hives, 4
Beer tumblers *see* Glasses, ale, beer
Bernal, Ralph, 22
Bigaglia, Pietro, 23
Bimann, Dominick, 18
Bird-fountains, 4
Birds, decorative use of, Pls. 44, 52, 62, 67
Birmingham glass industry, 6, 16, 24, 26, 61
Birmingham City Art Gallery, Elgin Vase, 42–3
Black
   glass tinted with, 16, 76, 81
   gold-decorated, 7
Blackfriars *see* Falcon glassworks
Blanc-de-lait glass, 62–3
Blottendorf, glass factory, 7
Blowing iron, 74
Blue, glass, painted, tinted with, 8, 9, 16, 18, 19, 57, 64, 76, Pls. 9, 42, 49, 52, 53, 66, 69, 70, 78, 79
B. Richardson (firm), 30
Boats, press-moulded, Pl. 73
Bohemia, glass from, 7–8, 19, 59, 74, 83
Bontemps, Georges, 9–10
Boston & Sandwich Glass Company, 52
Bott, Thomas, 47
Bottle glass, 2, 68; *see also* Bottles
Bottles
   cordial, 50
   Nailsea, 67
   ruby glass, Pl. 13
   scent, 49, Pls. 19, 21, 39, 43
   spirit, toilet, 4, 16
   water, 28, 36, 50
   wine, 6
Bowl and cover, Pl. 48
Bowls, finger, 4, 28

INDEX

Breakages, 51
Brierley Hill, cameo glass from, 46–7
Brierley Hill Public Library, Lecheverel cameo glass, 48
Bristol
  glass-makers' procession, 1738, 68
  rise, decline of glass industry, 6
Bristol blue glass, 9
British Cast Plate Manufacturers, 82
British Museum, glass collection, 35, 42, 43, 45, 74
Broad glass, 61, 74, 82
Brown, glass painted, tinted with, 16, 76, Pls. 17, 40, 61, 68
Bubbles, decorative use of, Pls. 75, 76
Bulls eye, 76–7
Buquoy, Count von, 7
'Burmese' glass, 55–6, Pls. 54, 55
Burne-Jones, Edward, 34
Burns, Robert, cameos of, 20
Busts, glass, 18 and Pl. 5; see also Cameos
Butter coolers see Coolers
Butter tubs see Tubs
Buttons, glass, 25–6 and Pl. 23

Caledonian Glass Works see Holyrood Flint Glass Works
Calotype photography, 15
Cameos, cameo glass
  'ivory' technique, 48 and Pl. 44
  moulded intaglios, 18
  origins, 74, 75
  plaque, Pl. 37
  production techniques, 19–20, 75, Pls. 35, 36
  revival of, 42–6, 59, 74–5
  scent bottles, Pl. 43
  Webb's, 47–8 and Pls. 38, 44
Cameras, glass for lenses, 10
Canary (yellow), glass tinted with, 16
Candelabra, Prince Albert's, 15–16
Candlesticks, Pl. 11
Cane, 75
Carafes, 4, 21, 57, Pls. 6, 20
Carbonate of potash, uses, 79–80
Carder, Frederick, 46
Casing, use with colour, cutting, 10, 75
Casting, of plate glass, 82
Castors, sets of, 4

Celery glasses, vases, see Glasses, Vases
Chair, of craftsmen, 75–6
Champagne glasses see Glasses
Chance, Hugh, 68
Chance, Robert Lucas, 9–10
Chance, William, 68
Chance Brothers, Birmingham, 6, 14
Chandeliers, 15–16, 18, 37 and Pl. 56
Chess tables, 18
Christy, J. F., 12, Pl. 6
Chrysoprase tinted glass, 16
Claret glasses, jugs, see Glasses, Jugs
Clarke, Samuel, 56; see also S. Clarke
Clichy, glassworks at, 24
Cloches, 67
'Clutha' glass, 65–6, Pl. 76
Cobalt, 76
Cole, Henry, 12
Colour
  in Bohemian glass, 7–8
  in 'Burmese' glass, 55
  in cameo glass, 43
  in glass lustres, 25
  in Venetian glass, 49
  increasing use by British glassmakers, 9–10, 16
  techniques for obtaining, 16, 51, 72, 76, 81
  use with cutting, casing, 10–11
  see also individual colours
Competition, intensity of, 30
Comports, press-moulded, Pl. 30
Compotiers, 16
Coolers
  butter, 16, 25
  wine, 4, 28
Copper oxide, 16, 51, 76
Corning Glass Works, 46
Cottage antiques, 78
Couper see James Couper and Sons
Cranberry (ruby) glass, 16, 18, 51–3, 76, Pls. 39, 47
Cream (colour), glass painted, tinted with, Pls. 15, 67
Cream basins, jugs, see Basins, Jugs
'Cribs', 3, 31, 32, 56–7
Crimping moulds, 76
Cristal opalin glass, 8
Cristallo see Venetian glass

INDEX

Crown glass, 61, 68, 74, 76-7, 78
Cruets, 4
Crutched Friars, early glassworks at, 6
Crystal, 77, 80
Crystal Palace, 14, 74
'Crystallo-ceramies' by Apsley Pellatt, 19-20, 75
Cullet, 3, 77, 80
Cups
  custard, jelly, 4-5
  finger, 4
  Nailsea, 67
Curiosities of Glassmaking, 1849, Apsley Pellatt, 21, 23
Curtain poles, 18
Custard cups *see* Cups
Cut glass, cutting techniques
  Bohemian, 74
  continuing fashion for, 4, 59, 66, 77
  described, 1, 77
  épergne, Pl. 1
  excessive, 6
  firms showing, at Great Exhibition, 16-17
  illustrated, Pls. 20, 21, 22
  in ruby glass, Pl. 14
  introduction, 77
  period of decline in demand, 45-6
  rivalry with engraving, 29
  'Rock Crystal', 59-60, 77-8, Pls. 61, 62
  use with casing, colour, 10-11, Pl. 11
  see also Engraved glass
Cutters, independent, 32
Czechoslovakia, glassmaking in, 7

Daguerrotype photography, 15
Dating, problems of, 7, 68, 70, 71
Davis Greathead & Green, 16, 30
Davidson *see* George Davidson & Co.
Davies, H. A., Pl. 43
Davis and Johnson, itinerant glass makers, 71
Debruge-Duménil, M., 21
Decanters, 4, 7, 10, 17, 19, 21, 28, 29, 50-1, 57, Pls. 3, 51, 57
Decorated-Opaque-Stained-Blanc-de-Lait glassware, 62-3
Dennis glassworks, Stourbridge, 45, 47; *see also* Thomas Webb

Dennis (Pegasus) Vase, 45, 47
Design, designs
  determining factors, 80
  efforts to improve standards, 11-13
  fashions in, 1-2, 7, 29, 30, 32-5, 55-66, Pls. 75, 76, 77
  from nature, Pls. 2, 6, 7, 12, 14, 20, 26, 28, 32, 34, 39, 40, 41, 62, 67
  identifying origins from, 7
  in cameo glass, 48-9
  in etched glass, 41, 42-3, 78
  in Nailsea glass, 68
  in press-moulded glass, 64-6
  in ruby glass, 51-3
  inspiration from Venice, 37, 49-51, 57-8, 59-60, 64-5, 83-4
  Morris's concept of, 37, 57
  pillar-moulding, 81-2
  pincering, 82
  see also Themes
Dessert services, 28
Dining Room, The, Mrs. Loftie, 49-51
Dinner services, 28
Dishes
  press-moulded, Pl. 64
  trifle, 4
Dobson & Pearce, London, 28, Pl. 26
Domes, French, 4-5
Door-knobs, 16, 25
Dossie, James, 9
Dresser, Christopher, 65-6, Pls. 76, 77
Drinking vessels, 7, 30; *see also individual types*
Drops, pincering of, 82; *see also* Lustres
Drum-sticks, Nailsea, 67
Duty *see* Taxation

Eastlake, Charles Locke, 36, 37
Edinburgh, glass industry in, 6, 20, 28
Edward Varnish & Co., 18, Pls. 10, 11
Egermann, Frederick, 7
Eisert, F., Pl. 24
Elgin marbles, 43
Elgin Vase, 42-3
Enamel
  various uses illustrated, Pls. 7, 16, 52
  vitrified, Pl. 17
  see also individual colours

INDEX

Engraved glass, engraving techniques
at Great Exhibition, 17–18
combination with etching, 41
continuing fashion for, 4, 59, 66
illustrated, Pls. 1, 24, 25, 26, 27, 28, 33, 63
period of decline in demand, 45–6
rivalry with heavy cutting, 29
'Rock Crystal', 59–60, 77–8, Pls. 61, 62
skills of Miller & Co., 28
techniques, 77–8
see also Cut glass
Ensell family, 5
Épergnes, 56–7, Pl. 1
Etching
combination with engraving, 41
fashion for, 30
techniques, designs, 40–1, 78, Pl. 34
'Etruscan' shape jugs, 17–18
Ewers, ruby glass, Pl. 14
Exeter College, Oxford, Chapel, 57
Export trade, 1, 61
Eye glasses, 4–5, 10

F. & C. Osler, 16, 17, 18, 28, Pl. 5
Fairy lamps, 38–9, Pls. 31, 55
'Fairy' nightlights, 56
Falcon glassworks, 6
Favenza, dealer in glass, 35–6
Ferns, inspiration from, 29, Pl. 32
Finger bowls *see* Bowls
Fire polishing, 78
Fish globes, 4–5
Flagons, Nailsea, 67
Flashing, 78
Flask, striped, Pl. 79
Flaxman, John, 45
Flint glass *see* Lead glass
Flower stands, holders, 36, 51, Pls. 55, 58, 63; *see also* Vases
Flowers, decorative use of, Pls. 7, 12, 14, 26, 34, 39, 40, 50, 55, 66
Foliage, decorative use of, Pls. 2, 6, 12, 14, 18, 20, 24, 28, 32, 35, 41, 42, 44, 46, 52, 61, 66, 67
Footmakers, 73
Ford, John, 6, 20, 28, Pl. 1; *see also* Holyrood Flint Glass Works
Fowke, Francis, 27

Fox, Charles T., and George, Pl. 13
France, glassmaking in, 5–6, 8, 23–4, 30, 61
Franco-Prussian War, 1859, 27
'French Rank', Nailsea, 68
Friggers, 69–70, 78
Fritsche, William, 60, Pl. 61
Frosted glass *see* Ice glass
Fruits, decorative use of, 54, Pls. 20, 26, 41, 42, 50, 55, 61
Functionalism, 34–5
Furnaces, 78

Gadgets, defined, 78–9, 82
Gaffers, 73
Gatchell, George, 17
Gateshead, glass works at, 62–3, 64; *see also* George Davidson & Co., Sowerby
Gathers, 72, 73
George III, King, 2
George Bacchus & Sons, 16, 22, 24, 79, Pls. 8, 9, 14, 17
George Davidson & Co., 64, Pl. 71
Germany, engravers from, 59
Giallo, tinted glass, 62–3
Gibbons, Sir Sillis John, Pl. 24
Gilding *see* Gold
Gladstone, W. E., 64
Glass *see* Glassmaking, Glassware and *under different types of glass*
Glasses
ale, beer, 4–5, 28
celery, 4
champagne, 4–5, 22, 28, Pl. 60
claret, 4–5, 28
finger, 4, 28
for lenses, 4–5, 10
hock, 4–5, 28
liqueur, 16, 28, 36
loop-stemmed, 22
pickle, 4
rum, 28
show, 4–5
soda-water, 28
wine, 4–5, 6, 10, 16, 21, 25, 28, 29, 36, 37, 51, Pls. 8, 9, 28, 29
Glasshouses *see* Furnaces, Glassmaking
Glassmaker's soap, 81
Glassmaking, glassmakers
ban on burning of wood, 5

competition in, 12–13, 30
conservatism, 4
cribs, 3, 31, 32, 56–7
furnaces, 78
health hazards, 47, 77
impetus from Crystal Palace, 14
independent cutters, 32
itinerant, 71
licensing of factories, 2
links between firms, families, 30–1
location, in Britain, 1, 5–6
organization, 31–2, 73, 75–6
processions, 68–9
Royal Commission on, 1833, 3–4, 8–9
techniques, 72–3, 74, 75–6
trade unionism in, 31, 68–9
trends in output, 3
Glassware
 availability of cheap, 24–5
 demand for English, Venetian compared, 37
 export trade, 1, 61
 fountains, 71
 friggers, 69–70
 imposition, repeal of tax, 1, 2–4, 8–9, 29–30, 77
 prices, 10, 40, 50
 second-hand, 25
 see also Design and under individual types of glassware
Globes, fish, 4–5
Glory hole, 73, 79
Goblets, 4–5, 7, 16, 18, 25, 28, Pls. 2, 10, 33
Gold, decoration with, 7, 10–11, 19, 25, 51, 55, 62–3, 74, Pls. 12, 14, 16, 23, 52
Gold, chloride, oxide of, 16, 51, 76
Gothic style, influence on design, 7, 11
Grapes, dish for, Pl. 65
Gratzen glass industry, 7, 74
Great Exhibition, 1851, 12, 14, 15–18, 22, 23–4, 32, 74, Pl. 8
Greathead, William, 30
Greek key pattern, 40
Green see J. G. Green
Green, glass painted, tinted with, 7, 8, 9, 16, 18, 19, 28, 57, 64, 67, 68, 76, Pls. 21, 42, 45, 48, 49, 56, 57, 69, 78
Green and Pellatt, 6

Greenaway, Kate, 52, 64, Pl. 67
Greener see Wear Glass Works
Gregory, Mary, 51–2
Grotesque, fashion for, 65–6, Pls. 75, 76, 77
Guest Brothers, Stourbridge, etched glass, 41–2
Guide du Verrier, Le, Georges Bontemps, 10
Guttery, D. R., 51, 56–7

Hale Thompson, F., 18
Hancocks (Hancox), Daniel, 43–4
Handbells, 78, Pl. 80
Handmaid to the Arts, The, James Dossie, 9
Hands, moulded, Pls. 65, 66
Harris see Rice Harris & Son
Hats, Nailsea, 67
Hawkes see Thomas Hawkes & Co.
Health, hazards to, in glassmaking, 47, 77
Heat-resistant glass, 28–9
Henry Greener & Co., Sunderland, 63–4
Henzey (Hennezel), glass-making family, 5
Hints on Household Taste, C. L. Eastlake, 36
Hock glasses see Glasses
Hodgetts, Richardson and Pargeter, 30
Holyrood Flint Glass Works, Edinburgh, 6, 20, 28, Pls. 1, 19, 27, 28
Honey, W. B., 79
Honey-pots, 16, 25
Hooman & Maliskeski, 38
Human figures, faces, depiction of, 49, 51–2
Hungary, glassmakers from, 5
Hungary Hill, Stourbridge, 5
Hyalith, in Bohemian glass, 7
Hydrochloric acid, use of, 51, 76
Hydrofluoric acid, use of, 40, 41, 44

Ice glass, 20–1, 79
Illustrated London News, 37–8
Ink, Exciseman's, 4–5
Inkstands, 4
Inscriptions, preservation by incrustation, 20
Intaglios
 hand-cut, 18
 moulded, 18
Ireland, glassmaking in, 1, 17
Iron oxide, use of, 76

Ivory cameo glass, 48, Pl. 44
Ivory Queen's Ware, 62-3

J. G. Green, London, 16-18, 28
Jackson, T. G., 57, Pl. 57
James I, King, 5
James Couper & Sons, Glasgow, 65-6, Pl. 76
James Powell and Sons, 2-3, 6, 18, 32, 37, 49-50, 57, Pls. 56, 57, 58, 59, 60
Japonaiserie, 54, 60, 64, 65-6
Jar and cover, ruby glass, Pl. 47
Jars, preserve, 36
Jelly cups *see* Cups
Jet, glass tinted to resemble, 62-3
Jewitt, Llewellyn, 42
Jugs
  'Ailsa', 28, Pl. 26
  claret, 16, 21, 28, 36, Pl. 24
  cream, 4, 21
  design trends, 29, 50, 51
  Dresser's, 66, Pl. 77
  'Etruscan' shape, 17-18
  illustrated, Pls. 18, 27
  Nailsea, 67
  'Neptune', 17
  press-moulded, 65, Pl. 75
  water, 4, 12, 16, 28, Pls. 7, 34, 77
Jukes, Tom, 56-7

Keller, Joseph, 60, Pl. 62
Ker & Co. *see* Andrew Ker & Co.
King's Lynn, glass from, 70
Kny, Frederick (?Ludwig), 59-60, Pl. 37

Labarte, Jules, 21
Lamps
  fairy, 38-9, Pls. 31, 55
  passage, 4-5
Lancet panels, in decanters, 7
Latticinio glass, 21, 54-5, 79
Layard, A. H. 36
Lead (flint) glass
  deep-cut, 1
  introduction, 1
  press-moulded, 61-2
  techniques for production, 23, 72-3, 79-80
  see also Glassmaking, Rock Crystal

Lead oxide, use of, 79, 80
Lecheverel, Alphonse-Eugène, 48
Leer ('lehr'), 73, 80-1
Lenses, glass for, 4-5, 10
Life of Josiah Wedgwood, The, Eliza Meteyard, 42
Life of Josiah Wedgwood, The, Llewellyn Jewitt, 42
Lilac (colour), glass tinted with, 8
Lime, as flux, 84
Liqueur glasses *see* Glasses
Litharge *see* Lead oxide
Lithyalin, in Bohemian glass, 7
'Little-goes', use of, 3
Lloyd & Summerfield, 16, 18
Locke, Joseph, 48
Loftie, Mrs., 49-51
London
  firms from, at Great Exhibition, 16-17
  International Exhibition, 1862, 27-9, 38, 43, Pl. 26
  International Health Exhibition, 1884, 47
  smoky atmosphere, 59
  see also Society of Arts, Victoria and Albert Museum
London Labour and the London Poor, Mayhew, 25
Lorraine, craftsmen from, 5, 30, 61
Lorraine process *see* Broad glass
Lustres, 25, 75, Pls. 22, 23

Macmillans' 'Art at Home' series, 49-51
Majolica, tinted glass, 62-3
Malachite, tinted glass, 62-3, 64
Management, organization of, 31-2
Manchester, glass industry in, 6, 16, 61
Manchester Town Hall, goblet engraved with, Pl. 33
Manganese, use of, 72, 76, 80, 81
Marbling, 7, Pl. 68
Marks, makers', patent, 63, 64
Marver, 73, 81
Matsu no ke, 54
Matt finish, fashion for, 18, 19
Mayhew, Henry, 25
Metal, in glassmaking, defined, 81
Meteyard, Eliza, 42
'Milk' glass *see* Opaline

INDEX

Milk-pans, 67
Millefiori, 23–4, 81
Miller & Co., Edinburgh, 28, 29, Pl. 28
Milton, John, bust of, 18
Minton's (china), 11–12
'Modern Painting on Glass', John Ruskin, 33–4
Molineux, Webb and Co., Manchester, 6, 16
Montecchi, Signor, 35
Moody, F., Pl. 25
Morris, William, 34, 37, 57, Pl. 29
Morris, Marshall, Faulkner & Co., 37
Mosaic, experiments with, 57–9
Moulded glass *see* Press-moulding
Mount Washington Glass Company, Massachusetts, 55
Mounts, for *opaline*, 8
Müller *see* Miller & Co.
Murano *see* Venice, Venetian glass
Museum of Ornamental Art, 22
Mustards, 4

Nailsea glass, 9, 67, 68
National Flint Glass Makers' Friendly Society of Great Britain and Ireland, 31
Neal and Tonks, Birmingham, 26
'Neptune Jug', 17
Neri, Antonio, 8
New York State, Corning Glass Works, 46
Newcastle on Tyne, glass industry, 6, 61–63, 68
Netherlands
  export of glass to, 61
  glass industry, 1
Nightlights, 56; *see also* Fairy lamps
Nitre, 80
Nitric acid, use of, 51, 76
Normandy glass *see* Crown glass
Northwood, John, 40–1, 42–6, 74–5, 77, 78
Northwood, John, Junior, 44–5, 46, 47, 52
Northwood, Joseph, 40

Oenochoë, inspiration from, 17–18, 29, 42
Off-white (colour), in *cristal opalin* glass, 8
'Old Roman' glass, 66
Opaline, opalescent glass, 8, 16, 19, 25, 62–3, 76, Pls. 18, 21, 49, 50, 51, 58, 71
Opaque glass, 7, Pls. 12, 15, 17, 36, 37, 42, 46, 53, 65, 70, 77
Osler *see* F. & C. Osler
Oxides, in making coloured glass, 16, 51, 72, 76, 80, 81

Painting, embellishment with, 10–11, 25, 74, Pls. 12, 14, 15, 16, 17, 23; *see also individual colours*
Paperweights, 23, 75, 81
Paraison, 73, 81
Pargeter, Philip, 43–4
Paris
  International Exhibition, 1867, 42
  International Exhibition, 1879, 48
  origins of cameo incrustation in, 75
Patent Office, 63
Pattern *see* Design
Paxton, Joseph, 14
Pearl ashes, 80
'Pearline' glass, 64
Peel, Robert, glass bust of, 18
Pegasus (Dennis) Vase, 45, 47
Pellatt, Apsley, Sr., 6, Pl. 3; *see also* Apsley Pellatt
Pellatt, Apsley, Jr., 19–21, 23, 79, 82
Pellatt and Green, 6
Pen-tray and stand, Pl. 73
Percival Vickers and Co., Ltd., Pl. 30
Photography
  records of Great Exhibition, 15
  use by John Northwood, 45
Pillar-moulding, 81–2
Pincering, 82
Pinching, 25–6
Pink, glass painted, tinted with, 8, 16, 57, 81, Pls. 9, 40, 41, 42, 48, 49, 54
Plaques, 20, Pls. 3, 37, 38
Plate glass, 75, 82
Plates
  ice, 28
  press-moulded, 61
Plymouth, glassmakers' procession, 1838, 68–9
Polishing *see* Cut glass
Pontil-marks, 70, 72, 79, 82
Portland Vase
  copies, 42, 43–4, 46, 48

INDEX

Portland Vase—*cont.*
  original, 42, 43, 74
Portraits, in glass, 18, Pls. 5, 19
Potash, use of, 60, 79–80
Potichomanie, 37–8
Powell, Harry J., 2, 3, 37, 57, 58, 69–70
Powells of Whitefriars *see* James Powell & Sons
Pre-Raphaelites, 34
Press-moulded glass
  bust of Queen Victoria, 18, Pl. 5
  development of, 10, 60–4, 78, 81, 82–3
  illustrated, Pls. 5, 30, 64, 65, 67, 68, 69, 70, 72, 73
  popularity, 25
Price (of glassware), 10, 40, 50
Printing, transfer-, Pl. 17
Prisms, 25
Procellas, 83
Prussia Street Flint Glassworks, Manchester, Pl. 33
Puce (colour), glass tinted with, 64
Pucellas *see* Procellas
Pugin, A. W. N., 11
Punty *see* Pontil-marks

'Queen's Burmese Ware', 55–6, Pls. 54, 55
Quilted glass (*verre de soie*), 55, 83

Raphael, grotesques, 28
Ravenscroft, George, 1, 22, 79
Red, glass painted, tinted with, 7, 76, Pls. 16, 49, 56, 61, 78, 79; *see also* Ruby glass
Redgrave, Richard, 11, Pl. 6
Rice Harris and Son, 16, 24, 25
Richardson, Benjamin, 9, 30, 48
Richardson, Jonathan, 9, 30
Richardson, William Haden, 9, 30
Richardson's Vitrified Glass, Pl. 7
Richmond, William Bruce, 58–9
Ridgways of Staffordshire, 20
Riedel, Josef, 7
'Rock Crystal', 59–60, 77, Pls. 61, 62
Rolling pins, 67, 78, Pl. 78
Rome, ancient
  cameo glass, 42, 74
  glass-making techniques, 23
  millefiori, 23–4, 81

pillar-moulding, 81–2
Portland Vase, 42, 43, 74
Rossetti, D. G., 34
Rothschild, Baron Gustave de, 22
Royal Commission on the Glass Industry, 3–4, 8–9
Royal Exchange, commemorative plaque, 20, Pl. 3
Ruby glass
  designs, patterns, 51–3
  fashion for, 16, 51
  illustrated, Pls. 12, 13, 23, 39, 47
  techniques for production of, 51, 52, 76
  Varnish's display of, 18
Rum glasses *see* Glasses
Ruskin, John, 33–4, 37, 65

St. Louis, glassworks at, 24
St. Paul's Cathedral, mosaics, 58–9
Salt cellars, 4, 16, 25, 36, 51
Saltpetre, 79, 80
Salviati, Antonio, 35, 36, 57–8
Sand, in lead glass, 79–80
Sander, George B., 10
Satin finish, Pls. 52, 53, 65
Satin glass (*verre de soie*), 55, 83
Scandinavia, export of glass to, 61
Scheibner, Frank, 60
Schreiber, Lady Charlotte, 35
S. Clarke's Fairy Patent Trademark, Pl. 55
Scotland, glass industry in, 6; *see also* Edinburgh, Holyrood Flint Glass Works
Scott, George Gilbert, 57–8
Scott, Walter, glass bust of, 18
Servitors, 73
Shakespeare, William, glass bust of, 18
Shape *see* Design
Shaw, Norman, 36
Shears, 83
Sheet glass (Crown, Broad glass), 6, 9–10, 61, 67, 68, 74, 76–7, 78, 82
Ships, glass, 71
Shirley, Frederick S., 55
Show glasses *see* Glasses
Silhouettes, in ruby glass, 52
Silvered glass, Varnish's patent, 18, Pls. 10, 11
Silverware, 1–2
Slade, Felix, 35

INDEX

Slag glass, 62
Smethwick, Chance's factory at, 9
Smith, John, of Leith, Pl. 27
Smithsonian Institution, Washington, 45
Society of Arts, 11-12, 21-2, 24, 27-9
Soda, in glassmaking, 23, 60, 80, 84
South Kensington Museum, 35
Southwark *see* Apsley Pellatt & Co.
Sowerby & Neville (Sowerby & Co., Sowerby's Ellison Glass Works), 62-63, 65, Pls. 67, 68, 69, 70, 72, 74, 75
Spirit bottles *see* Bottles
Staffordshire House, Truro, 5
Stangate Glass Works, Lambeth, Pl. 6
Steuben (later Corning) Glass Works, 46
Stevens & Williams, Brierley Hill, 46, 54, 60
Stevens & Williams Patent Art Glass, Pls. 39, 62
Stone, Benjamin, 42
Stone, Fawdry & Stone, 42
Stones of Venice, The, John Ruskin, 33-4
Storr, Paul, 1
Stourbridge, glass industry in, 5-6, 8-9, 12, 16, 29-30, 40, 45, 59-60; *see also* individual firms
Sugar basins, vases *see* Basins, Vases
'Sulphides', by Apsley Pellatt, 19-20; *see also* Cameos
Summerly's Art Manufactures, 12, Pl. 6
Sunderland *see* Wear Glass Works

Table centrepiece, Pl. 55; *see also* Épergnes
Taker in, 73
Tape-designs, Pl. 48
Tatham, Charles Heathcote, 2
Taxation of glassware, imposition, removal, 1, 2-4, 8-9, 29-30, 77
Tazzas, 16, 36
Teams Glass Works, Gateshead, 64
Themes, depiction of biblical, classical, Pls. 15, 16, 17, 18, 27, 36
Thomas Hawkes & Co., Dudley, 30-1
Thomas Webb & Sons, Stourbridge, 16, 37, 47-8, 55-6, 59-60, 66, Pls. 32, 38, 44, 55
Thorpe, W. A., 78
Thread designs, 16, 55, 79, 84, Pls. 9, 45
Toilet bottles *see* Bottles

Topaz (colour), glass tinted with, Pls. 48, 51, 58
Torr, Cecil, 38
Tortoise Shell Ware, 62-3
Trade Unionism in glass industry, 31, 68-9
Transfer-printing, Pl. 17
Trapped air patterns, 83
Trifle dishes *see* Dishes
True Principles of Pointed or Christian Architecture, A. W. N. Pugin, 11
Truro, Staffordshire House, 5
Tubs, butter, 4
Tumblers, 4-5, 10, 16, 21, 25, 28, 29, 36, 50, 51, 61, 66, Pl. 77
Turner, J. M. W., 34
Turquoise (colour), glass tinted with, 16, 62-3
Tyzack (Thisack) family, 5

United Flint Glass Cutters, 31
Uranium oxide, 55
Uranium, salt of, 9, 76
Ure, Andrew, 75, 77

Varnish, Edward, 18
'Vaseline' glass, 76, Pl. 71
Vases
  at Great Exhibition, 16
  celery, 28, Pl. 32
  decoration by casing, 75
  decoration by Potichomanie, 37-8
  flower, 36, 51, Pls. 51, 55, 58, 63, 66
  in 'Burmese' ware, 56, Pl. 54
  opal glass, 19
  press-moulded, 64-5, Pls. 68, 69
  Rock Crystal, Pl. 62
  ruby glass, Pl. 12
  sugar, 28
  various, illustrated, Pls. 12, 14, 15, 16, 17, 35, 36, 40, 42, 44, 46, 50, 52, 67, 74, 76
  Venetian glass, 36
Venetian glass
  ice glass, 79
  inspiration from, 35, 49, 57-8, 59-60, 62-3, 64-5, Pls. 8, 9, 59, 60
  milk glass, 8
  production techniques, 23, 60, 80, 83-4
  reproduction, 35-6, 83-4

INDEX

Venetian glass—*cont.*
  revival of interest in, 21-2
  revival of output, 35
Verre de soie, 55, 83
Vickers *see* Percival Vickers & Co.
Victoria, Queen, 2, 6, 18, 55-6, 64, Pls. 1, 3, 5, 64, 72
Victoria and Albert Museum, 22, 35, 37, 42, 47-8, Pl. 38
Vienna, exhibition of *millefiori*, 1845, 23
Vitro-Porcelain tinted glass, 62-3

Walking sticks, 67, 78
Walpole, Horace, 1-2
Warrington, glass from, 61
Water bottles, jugs *see* Bottles, Jugs
Waterford glass, 1
Watson, Rosamund Marriott, 66
Watts, G. F., 58
Wear Glass Works, Sunderland, 63-4
Webb, Philip, 57, Pl. 29
Webb, Thomas, 30, 47
Webb, Thomas Wilkes, 45
Webb *see also* Thomas Webb
Wedgwood, Josiah, 42, 43, 45
Wellington, Duke of, 20, Pl. 19
Westminster Abbey, reredos, 57-8

W. H. B. & J. Richardson, 9, 16, 30, 40, 43, 48, Pls. 7, 15, 16, 18
White, glass painted, tinted with, 19, 76, Pls. 9, 40, 48, 49, 68, 78, 79; *see also* Opaque glass
Whitefriars *see* James Powell
William III, King, 2
William IV, King, 2
Window glass, 6, 9-10, 61, 67, 68, 74, 76-8
Wine bottles, coolers, glasses *see* Bottles, Coolers, Glasses
Witch-balls, 78
Woodcuts, records of glass shown at Great Exhibition, 15
Woodall, George, 47, 48, Pls. 36, 38, 43
Woodall, Thomas, 47, 48
Worcester porcelain, 47
Wordsley, Northwoods' works at, 40, 46-7
Wordsley School of Art, 46
Wright and Mansfield, 42

Yellow, glass painted, tinted with, 7, 8, 9, 76, Pls. 40, 41, 48, 49, 52, 54, 61, 71

Zach, of Munich, 43